HISTORY *of* FURNITURE

Ancient to 19th C.

HISTORY *of* FURNITURE

Ancient to 19th C.

Michael Huntley

GUILD OF MASTER CRAFTSMAN PUBLICATIONS

This collection first published 2004 by
Guild of Master Craftsman Publications Ltd
Castle Place, 166 High Street
Lewes, East Sussex BN7 1XU

ISBN 1 86108 319 X

A catalogue record for this book is available from the British Library.

Publisher: Paul Richardson
Art Director: Ian Smith
Production Manager: Hilary MacCallum
Managing Editor: Gerrie Purcell
Editor: Olivia Underhill
Designer: Jo Patterson
Illustrator: Rob Wheele

Set in Berkeley, Trajan and Syntax

Colour origination by Icon Reproduction (cover), MRM Graphics (book)
Printed and bound by Kyodo Printing, Singapore

CONTENTS

Foreword
Introduction

CHAPTER ONE   ANCIENT AND OAK

CHAPTER TWO   THE AGE OF ENLIGHTENMENT

CHAPTER THREE   THE TWILIGHT OF CRAFTSMANSHIP

CHAPTER FOUR CHAIRS AND THE 19TH CENTURY

CHAPTER FIVE THE VICTORIAN ERA AND ARTISTIC REVIVAL

FOREWORD

Antique furniture can be viewed as one of the most robust forms of historical document, and most tangible of links with our forebears. When we learn how to read this three-dimensional information it reveals as much as any book can about the art, technology, philosophy and aspirations of the age in which a piece was made.

It is interesting to note the cyclical nature of ideas and fashions in furniture design – a good example being the Gothic style, introduced from ecclesiastical architecture in the 12th century and revived in the mid-18th and again in the early 19th centuries. Reaction to political events such as revolution or counter-revolution is clearly identifiable, often resulting in abrupt rejection of the preceding aesthetic values – perhaps in favour of simplicity at first, followed by over-ornamentation or the resurrection of earlier ideas, as in the case of mid-17th-century English furniture.

Artistic representation of natural forms has been part of furniture ornamentation since the earliest times: first as simple chip-carved work, then developing to the highest levels of naturalistic sculptural carving. New and relatively complex technologies were quickly adopted to decorate furniture, such as gilding, scagliola and marquetry, confirming furniture as a symbol of status and taste just as much as fine clothing or a grand house. It is fascinating to see the combination of art and science and the balance of form and function at play in the design of furniture through the ages. This book takes the reader on an exciting pictorial journey through the development of furniture; progressing rapidly from era to era, it makes comparisons and contrasts easily recognizable and understandable.

I commend Michael for his diligence and skill in selecting images from Sotheby's photographic archive which so clearly illustrate the evolution of furniture in such a concise way, to the enlightenment of all readers.

Adrian Smith MVO, ACR

INTRODUCTION

My position as Head of Furniture Restoration and Conservation at Sotheby's gave me access to the huge number of photographs of pieces of furniture that have been taken over the years for Sotheby's catalogues. When Paul Richardson, Publisher at GMC Publications, asked me if I would like to write a short history of furniture to be illustrated by some of these photographs, Sotheby's kindly agreed to let us use the images and Paul and I set about designing a series of 12 articles for *Furniture & Cabinetmaking* magazine. The work began in 1999. Five hundred photographs later I had reached 1900!

This was a project that grew and grew. Thanks to Sotheby's we have been able to publish a massive archive of colour photographs which are reproduced in as close to chronological order as printing constraints will allow. Although the photographs were loaned by Sotheby's the text is my responsibility. I have tried to write with conservators and restorers in mind, rather than academics. I have therefore made generalizations that I hope give an overview of the periods and styles concerned, without delving into deep and abstruse art history and research. The value of this work lies in the images and the continuous picture that they give of the development of furniture in the Western world for the last five hundred years. Woodworkers tend to 'see' rather than read. I hope that the images will provide woodworkers with a visual stimulation which is often missing in more wordy publications.

In some of the early chapters we have had to use drawings where original photographs were not available. I hope that we have done justice to the originators of those early images from paintings and books. My thanks go to the Directors of Sotheby's, past and present, members of the Sotheby's Photographic and Furniture Departments, Archivists and Administrators and to private individuals who have allowed us to use images from their collections. I would also like to thank my colleagues both in the Conservation and Restoration Department at Sotheby's and in the various auction houses that I have worked in over the years, with whom I have had many enjoyable and lengthy discussions about the origin of pieces of furniture.

Finally I would like to thank GMC Publications for making this collection possible, and my wife Sue, who has put up with small mountains of photographs dotted around the house and who has read and re-read the entire text.

Michael Huntley ACR, FRSA

CHAPTER

ONE

Ancient and Oak

ANCIENT FURNITURE
1350 BC – AD 200

It may be thought that basic vernacular furniture such as chairs, tables, beds, chests and boxes were developed in the apparently settled period after the Normans invaded England. In fact, such items were being made in Egypt 2,500 years earlier. *Fig 1.1a* shows the interior of the ante-chamber of the tomb of Tutankhamun which dates from about 1350 BC. The room contains a mass of artefacts made from wood and other materials.

Left: Fig 1.1a **The interior of the ante-chamber of the tomb of Tutankhamun which dates from about 1350 BC.**

Below: Fig 1.1b **Wall painting from the tomb of Vizier Rekhmire in Thebes on the Nile showing chair-makers and carvers.**

ROYAL FURNITURE

The joints used would be familiar to any 20th-century cabinetmaker. Mortices and tenons were used to join legs and rails, cane was used to support seats and mattresses, and both dowels and nails were utilized. Right-angle joints were mitred and dovetails employed.

Royal furniture was inlaid with mother-of-pearl and ivory, and decorated with gold foil. Of course it was better made and better decorated than vernacular furniture – most of the population would probably have had little or no furniture at all. This means then, that our evidence is from the top end of the market where furniture has survived from the royal tombs and those of dignitaries.

CHAIR-MAKING

The wall painting from the tomb of Vizier Rekhmire in Thebes on the Nile, *see Fig 1.1b*, shows chair-makers and carvers. The man drilling holes for cane in the rails of the chair is undertaking an action that is familiar to any present-day furniture craftsman. The legs of the chair are clearly shown, cut out with the tenons at the top and hoof

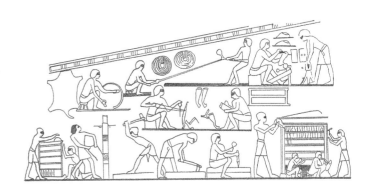

> " *Royal furniture was inlaid with mother-of-pearl and ivory, and decorated with gold foil* "

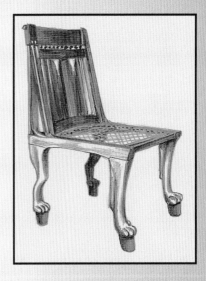

Above: Fig 1.1c **Marble relief carved with the figure of a man seated on a folding stool.**

Right top: Fig 1.1d **Both this chair and the one in Fig 1.1b are the antecedents of furniture in the French Directoire style of the late 18th century.**

Right centre: Fig 1.1e **A klismos chair with sabre legs, depicted on a gravestone dating from the 5th century BC.**

Right bottom: Fig 1.1f **Cabinet dating from 1350 BC.**

or paw feet at the base. There is a chair in the Louvre in Paris, *see Fig 1.1d*, which is very similar to that in the wall painting. Both these chairs are the antecedents of furniture in the French Directoire style of the late 18th century. The Directoire style developed, as will be detailed in a later article in the series, from the discoveries in Egypt, made in the last quarter of the 18th century.

TIMBER

Timbers used were the locally grown acacia, 'sycamore fig', tamarisk and sidder, although others such as cedar, cypress and juniper were imported from Syria. *Dalbergia melanoxylon* was used as ebony. Since the native trees could not provide decent-sized boards, jointing was developed using tongues or pegs. Veneers were used as decoration and in multi-ply construction which required glue – the existence of an animal glue is evidenced by their use of gesso.

FINE WORK

If anyone doubts the ability of the craftsman of two thousand years ago to produce detailed and fine work, just look at the cabinet in *Fig 1.1f*. This cabinet dates from 1350 BC, but similar cabinets are illustrated in wall paintings at the archaeological site of Saqqara, circa 2650 BC.

The framework is ebony, the panels are cedar, and the hieroglyphs are incised and filled with yellow pigment – a technique of decoration used two thousand years later in the 'heyday' of antique furniture in Europe. I use inverted commas, because this study has shown me that few techniques are new or unique to any craftsperson or period. The excellence of craftsmanship exhibited by the ancient Egyptians certainly appears, within the limitations of tooling, to be comparable to anything produced since.

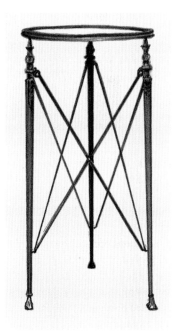

Above: Fig 1.1g **A painted vase depicts an X-frame stool with a head carved at the junction between the legs and the stretcher. 'Greek key' decoration is used on the frieze.**

Right: Fig 1.1h **Metal table from the Hildesheim Treasure, State Museum, Berlin.**

GREEK AND ROMAN

We must move on now to the Greek and Roman period without having the space to do justice to the furniture that was produced in the thousand years between Tutankhamun and the early Greeks. Our knowledge of Egyptian furniture is based on the evidence contained in tombs – both actual articles and wall paintings. The Greek and Roman evidence consists of hardly any actual objects, but there is a considerable body of writing, together with furniture shown in painted and sculpted interior decorations.

CHAIRS AND STOOLS

Chairs and stools began to look familiar: *Fig 1.1e* on page 13 shows a klismos chair with sabre legs, depicted on a gravestone dating from the 5th century BC. The marble relief shown in *Fig 1.1c* on page 13 is carved with a man seated on a folding stool. A painted vase shown in *Fig 1.1g* shows an X-frame stool with a head carved at the junction between the legs and the stretcher. 'Greek key' decoration is used on the frieze.

An interesting prototype of the Lloyd Loom chair is shown in *Fig 1.1i*. This is a wicker-work chair in which a Roman woman is having her hair dressed. The figure on the right is holding a mirror made from highly burnished metal. The relief dates from the 3rd century AD, and is displayed in Trier Museum.

INLAY AND INTARSIA

Inlay and intarsia were used extensively in Classical times. The word intarsia is derived from the Latin *interserere*, to insert. Ulysses describes to Penelope the bride bed which he had made: *"Beginning from the head post…I made it fair with inlaid work of gold, and of silver and of ivory."*

The woods used by the Greeks were ebony, cypress, cedar, oak, yew, holly, elder root, poplar, willow, olive, box, Corsican ebony, beech, Syrian terebinth, maple, palm (cut transversely for veneer), lotus and citron. This last was a timber highly prized for its figure and the Romans had special names for the particular patterns such as tigrinae, with tiger-like markings, and apiata, which is like 'parsley' wood, just as we have for special names for mahogany.

Pliny says that Cicero spent 500,000 sesterces just for one table. Half a million sesterces might be equivalent to US$35,000 or GB£20,000 at today's rate. This shows that having fashionable objects and fine furniture was as desirable then as it is now. Except that I wish I had been paid so generously for the last table that I made!

Left: Fig 1.1i **An interesting prototype of the Lloyd Loom chair dating from the 3rd century** AD.

Above: Fig 1.1j **Stucco ceiling which dates from about** AD 200.

ROOM SETTINGS

Circular tables were popular, either as fixed-leg tables or folding, as in the example of a metal table from the Hildesheim Treasure, State Museum, Berlin, shown in *Fig 1.1h*.

A curious opportunity to view a Roman room is given to us by the carving of the interior of a stone sarcophagus in the form of a room setting, *see Fig 1.1k*. This shows a console table against the wall and two cupboards with panelled doors and shelves. The Roman Empire provided the means for all this 'modern and fashionable' furniture to be spread around the known world, and it is on these basic forms that most historical furniture that we now encounter has been designed.

As a final thought, consider the stucco ceiling shown in *Fig 1.1j* which dates from about AD 200. The craftsmen of antiquity could produce work every bit as fine and graceful as those of England or France in the 18th century.

> " *A curious opportunity to view a Roman room is given to us by the carving of the interior of a stone sarcophagus in the form of a room setting* "

Above: Fig 1.1k **The drawing depicts a carving of the interior of a stone sarcophagus in the form of a room setting showing a console table against the wall and two cupboards with panelled doors and shelves.**

DARK AGES
MID 5TH – LATE 9TH C.

Above: Fig 1.2a **Throne in carved ivory, dated to the 6th century** AD, **can be found today in the Museo Arcivescovile in Ravenna.**

Having looked at ancient civilizations, we now enter the Dark Ages – no, not because I have fused all the lights in my workshop by trying out some massively powerful piece of ancient machinery, but because the Goths have arrived.

Rather sadly, the Gothic style is named after the Goths who are popularly thought of as wreckers of civilization. In fact, the style is named after a later attempt to imagine what the Goths were like – and the 'wreckers of civilization' were in fact not as bad as they were made out to be – they were only one among several tribes who invaded the crumbling Roman Empire.

As far as woodwork is concerned, this period suffers from having little evidence left behind. However, the Scandinavians were prodigious woodworkers who made trade routes from the Baltic to the Black Sea, from where they visited Byzantium, the new capital of the Eastern Empire, which is now Istanbul. Some wooden objects have been found in Viking archaeological sites.

All the methods of woodworking mentioned in the previous section were still in existence. Workshops do not just disappear when an invader arrives – craftsmen are one of the first trades to recover because the new aristocracy need fine goods in order to impress, just as much as the old order did.

BYZANTINE AND ROMANESQUE
The plain surfaces of Greek and Roman decorative art gave way to an abundance of formal surface decoration. Again, the name given to the decorative style is confusing. The Roman Empire in the Western Mediterranean had collapsed, but the Eastern Empire continued. The style of decoration that is associated with the Eastern Empire, whose capital was Byzantium, is called Byzantine or Romanesque. The Classical Roman Empire had vanished, but the name persisted in this way, even though Roman design standards consisted of

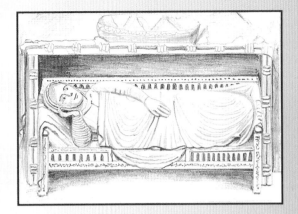

PRECISION JOINTS

In *Fig 1.2d* you will see a depiction in stone of the Virgin seated on a turned chair with tracery sides; the carving is 12th century. If the scale of the carving is accurate, the precision for the joints required was similar to that on a Gillows dressing stool made 500 years later. The carving is in La Charité-sur-Loire, Nièvre, France.

Next, let us look at a piece of stone carving at Chartres Cathedral, *see Fig 1.2c*, showing a nativity scene – the Virgin lies in a bed made of squared timber decorated with chip carving, the uprights terminating in turned spheres. This carving also dates from the 12th century and yet is as elegant and functional as a piece of Arts and Crafts furniture.

Above: Fig 1.2b **A simple monastic chair from the 12th century – the main structural members are square in form with arcaded decoration and a stylized hoof foot.**

Top right: Fig 1.2c **The Virgin is depicted lying in a bed made of squared timber decorated with chip carving, the uprights of which terminate in turned spheres, in this 12th-century carving.**

Bottom right: Fig 1.2d **Stone carving from the 12th century in which the Virgin is seated on a turned chair with tracery sides – the precision for the joints required was similar to that on a Gillows dressing-stool made 500 years later.**

simple, plain surfaces. The senators and centurions would have hated the overabundance of decoration on Byzantine or Romanesque objects.

MANUSCRIPT ILLUSTRATIONS

Byzantine and Romanesque furniture can be found depicted in illuminated manuscripts which were produced in an area that extended from Ireland to the Black Sea and from Scotland to Alexandria. The manuscripts often show an evangelist seated on a grand chair or 'throne'. There is little pre-first-millennium furniture extant, so these rather stilted pictures are useful as evidence of competent cabinetwork and design in the so-called Dark Ages. However, one such throne does exist – it is in the Museo Arcivescovile, in Ravenna, *see Fig 1.2a*. The throne is made from carved ivory and is dated

Left: Fig 1.2e **Drawing showing the prow of the Oseberg Ship, a burial ship for a queen from the 9th or 10th century – demonstrating considerable craftsmanship.**

PERIODS IN TIME

AD 476 – AD 1200	Byzantine
AD 500 – AD 1100	Romanesque
AD 1100 – AD 1500	Gothic
AD 1400 – AD 1600	Renaissance

As with all matters academic, these dates are open to dispute by various different authorities.

STYLES

Byzantine
Byzantine was a debased Roman style with profuse ornamentation inclining towards Near Eastern style. It was to be seen in later periods influencing Russian, South European and some Italian work.

Romanesque
Romanesque was a European style which came about after the fall of the Roman Empire. It followed the debased Roman style, was stiff and 'barbaric', and used stylistically rendered animal and plant forms.

Gothic
To the Romans, the word Gothic conjured up pictures of the barbarians of the North. To the Renaissance commentator the name implied the un-classical rudely home-made efforts of the Dark Ages when craftsmen forsook classic art in favour of solid, ecclesiastically inspired functionality. To the modern commentator the Gothic is regarded as having the primary greatness of a complete, spontaneous art system.

to the 6th century AD. The figures are taken from the life of Christ and the rails are decorated with foliage, vines, birds and mammals – this is a stunning piece of furniture that is 1,500 years old.

WRITING SLOPES
A much simpler 12th-century chair is shown in *Fig 1.2b* on page 17. The monk, Lawrence of Durham, is shown writing on parchment. The main structural members of the chair are square in form with arcaded decoration and a stylized hoof foot. The manuscript on which Lawrence is working is supported by a cantilevered arm. This arrangement looks very uncomfortable, but so many of the manuscripts show writing slopes of a Heath-Robinson type that one must assume that book supports were an important requirement for monastic chairs, and were much used.

BOOKS
Another point that should be made in relation to manuscripts is that the front and back boards of parchment books were made of thin sheets of planed wood – many of these end-boards are still in existence. This means that timber that was thicknessed to ¼in (6mm) or less, which is perhaps 900 years old, is sitting quietly in our great libraries! If anyone doubts the skill of the woodworkers of the so called Dark Ages, let them ask a bookbinder.

Below: Fig 1.2f **A decorated sledge, from the same burial – now 1,000 years old.**

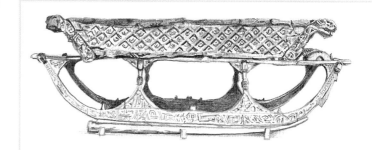

Right: Fig 1.2g **A suite of furniture from Gotland in Sweden dating from the 13th century – the structure is similar to English Tudor furniture.**

Below: Fig 1.2h **Taken from a manuscript from around** AD 700 **– the low table on the right has many features of modern-day furniture.**

SCANDINAVIA

Now let us turn north east and look at Scandinavian woodwork. This is an area that is often overlooked in woodworking history – which is quite wrong because the Scandinavian countries probably have a more comprehensive woodworking culture than that of southern Europe. It has been suggested that Viking woodwork was primitive and coarse – but if you look at *Fig 1.2e* you will see the prow of the Oseberg Ship, a burial ship for a queen from the 9th or 10th century – the shape is graceful and the thinness of the entwined lines indicates considerable ability. I think the skill of the craftsmen creating such work was far from primitive.

A decorated sledge, from the same burial, is shown in *Fig 1.2f*. This sledge is now 1,000 years old. It may not have been intended to be used on the snow, and may therefore be somewhat fanciful, but even so, the person who designed and made it was quite capable of producing elegant and desirable furniture as well as ships and paraphernalia of war.

COMPLEX FORMS

A suite of furniture dating from the 13th century is shown in *Fig 1.2g*. The structure is very similar to that found in English Tudor furniture – but these pieces come from Gotland in Sweden. They were not made for a 'great house', but are the sort of items that would have been found in a merchant's house. The forms are quite complex in terms of the number of joints used – as many as 42 in the chair, which is about average for a Georgian chair – but the decoration consists of plain turnings and incized lines. It is probably comparable to what we now call 'Provincial furniture'.

DECORATION

From records, we know about other items of Romanesque furniture including chests, cupboards and all sorts of boxes. Boxes were covered in leather, encrusted in ivory or other decorative organic and inorganic materials, sometimes painted or inlaid with various woods – who said Tonbridgeware was new? – and made with sophisticated locks. Incidentally, locks had, at that time, been around for at least 2,000 years.

ANCIENT OR MODERN

The final illustration, *Fig 1.2h*, is taken from the Codex Amiatinus, an ancient manuscript from around AD 700. The cupboard in the background has panelled doors with a red interior – on the right is a low table which has legs and stretchers – much like modern tables found in trendy furnishing stores!

MIDDLE AGES 1000 – 1350

" *Carpenters of the time had a thorough understanding of joint cutting* "

The Middle Ages, which is the period from about AD 1000 to about AD 1500, is a time that we know considerably more about than the preceding eras – and far more objects and pictures have survived, providing evidence for us.

BEST SELLER

Probably the 'best seller' of the Middle Ages was the trunk or chest. In its simplest form it was a hollowed-out tree trunk with a lid – *Fig 1.3a* shows a 'dug-out' chest of this type. There are a few such chests still in existence and they were, until the 1970s, to be found in the place that had been the home of much early furniture for 500 years or so – the English village church. Sadly, many of these churches were robbed, and it became necessary to move valuable items to museums or lock them away. However, the serious and determined student of antiquities can contact the church

verger who will generally be happy to arrange a viewing – county archivists will be able to tell you which pieces of furniture are with which churches.

CHEST DEVELOPMENT

In *Fig 1.3b* we see a 13th-century chest. The timber has been riven into slabs and held together with pegs. This made the whole piece appear lighter, and by making the corner posts into distinct legs, raised it and its contents up off the, probably damp, floor. Although this may look crude, buildings and ships from the same, and indeed earlier, periods reveal that the carpenters of the time had a thorough understanding of joint cutting. The lock on this chest is missing.

CARVING

Another chest is shown in *Fig 1.3c*. Here the chip-carved decoration, which harks back to Norse work, has given way to figurative decoration. It is not the formal stylized decoration of the Romanesque type, but is akin to the

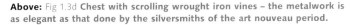

Above: Fig 1.3d **Chest with scrolling wrought iron vines – the metalwork is as elegant as that done by the silversmiths of the art nouveau period.**

Right: Fig 1.3e **A late 15th-century chest.**

Right middle: Fig 1.3f **Coronation chair – used at every English coronation since that of Edward II in 1308.**

Right bottom: Fig 1.3g **Coffer-maker's chair made from leather and timber.**

freedom of the medieval carvings that decorated the great churches and cathedrals – with figures taken from real life and immortalized in misericords, rood screens, and altar pieces all over the country. The carvers competed, as decorators, with the great painters of the day – wood was the medium on which they both worked, for even painters had to rely on wooden panels for a durable surface.

DECORATION

The chest in *Fig 1.3d* is covered with scrolling wrought iron. The similarity between this decoration and that found on church and castle doors from the 13th century is obvious. I include it as a tribute to the metalworkers of the period – the skill of these men, who made iron 'vines' as elegantly as the art nouveau silversmiths, should not be ignored.

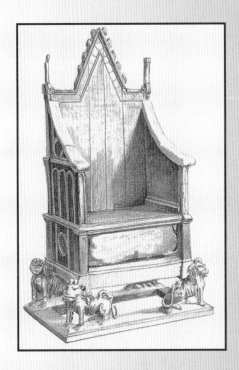

FAMOUS CHAIR

If the best seller in the Middle Ages was the chest, the most famous item of the era must be the Coronation Chair in Westminster Abbey, **see Fig 1.3f**. It has been used at every coronation since that of Edward II in 1308. The chair was made in oak by Master Walter, the king's painter, in 1300 to 1301 – we can be that precise because the account books, recording the payment of 100 shillings, still exist. Originally, the chair was covered in gesso, decorated overall with pricked geometric designs and foliage, and finally gilded. The lion-supports at the base are later additions, and the pinnacles on the crest rail have had their original surmounts of turrets and leopards removed.

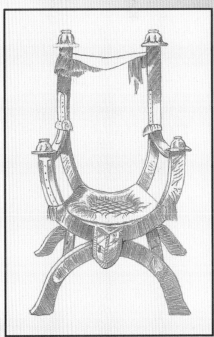

.ȷ rȷiu bmouun apfeu ȷiou. ralem rrubuaone rr
nprane pauirumbilibus.

Left: Fig 1.3h **Taken from a 13th-century manuscript, this illustration shows a monk seated on a turned chair with a woven seat and back.**

" *Towards the end of this period new designs began to filter through from Europe, together with the splitting apart of the woodworking crafts into those of carpenter, joiner and turner* "

The chest in *Fig 1.3e* on page 21 dates from the late 15th century and can be seen in the Victoria and Albert Museum, London. The trailing leaf decoration is typically English and bears similarities to the 'green man' carvings often found as roof bosses or capitals in ecclesiastical buildings.

STOOLS AND BENCHES

During the Middle Ages, wooden stools and benches continued to be used as the main form of seating. They were made by carpenters, using the same sort of design and

BASKET-WORK CHAIRS

I think it is worth mentioning basket-work chairs – they would have been used by merchants and other well-off, but non-aristocratic people, for many centuries. There is a 3rd-century carving in the Archaeological Museum in York, England showing a woman seated on a 'wanded' chair which is of a design that must have continued for many years, although no actual examples exist.

Basket makers are recorded as working in the 15th century in the City of London.

construction that was used in timber-framed buildings of the time – rebates, mortice and tenon, and pegged joints.

Towards the end of this period new designs began to filter through from Europe, together with the splitting apart of the woodworking crafts into those of carpenter, joiner and turner.

COFFER-MAKER'S CHAIR

There are two other forms of chair that should be mentioned – the coffer-maker's chair, *see Fig 1.3g on page 21*, and the turner's chair. The cofferer made boxes with timber carcasses which were covered in decorative leather – which more or less held the box together. He also made chairs from timber and leather – the example shown in *Fig 1.3g* has the basic X-frame stool form which we came across earlier, *see page 14*, but with improvements. The rear legs have been extended to form back supports and the front legs raised up to form arm supports. Various parts have had leather webs and padding added to make the whole thing far more comfortable.

TURNER'S CHAIR

A discussion of the turner's chair raises all sorts of questions about the role of the lathe in furniture history. I will not go into detail about this, except to say that it has probably been seriously undervalued by historians and theoreticians.

Right: Fig 1.3i **Copyist working at a complicated writing or copying desk made, it would appear, from quarter-sawn oak.**

Fig 1.3h, taken from a 13th-century manuscript, shows a monk seated on a turned chair with a woven seat and back, which was probably made of basket work. As in the similar illustration in the previous section, *see page 17*, the monk is using a 'Heath Robinson' type of book-rest. It is amazing to think that such a contrivance was being used to support a manuscript that might, in today's terms, be worth hundreds of thousands of pounds.

DESK AND CHAIR

The final illustration, *Fig 1.3i*, shows a copyist in his cell in the 15th century. Copying was a perfectly reasonable thing to do at the time – it was the only way that extra copies of

books could be made, and it also ingrained the contents of the book in the copyist's mind. He is seated in a chair with turned rails and legs, at a complicated writing or copying desk made, it would appear, from quarter-sawn oak. These illustrations have been copied from original ancient manuscripts. There is far more detail, such as the grain of the timber, in the originals which can be seen as photographic illustrations in the appropriate museum catalogues. In the corners of the picture are a small bench or stool and a domed-top coffer.

RELEVANT DATES

Saxon & Norman	10th, 11th and 12th centuries	
Edward the Confessor	1042–1066	Westminster Abbey, London began to be built
Harold II	1066–1066	Battle of Stamford Bridge in which Harold beat off an invasion from the Vikings
William the Conqueror	1066–1087	Battle of Hastings in which Harold lost to William – Domesday Book compiled
William II (Rufus)	1087–1100	William II killed in a hunting accident at Rufus Stone in the New Forest, in the south of England. You can still visit the spot where he is said to have died
Stephen	1135–1154	
Plantagenet Kings	mid 12th, 13th, 14th and 15th centuries	
Henry II	1154–1189	Thomas á Becket murdered
Richard I	1189–1199	Richard the Lionheart and Robin Hood
John	1199–1216	Magna Carta
Edward I	1272–1307	Prince of Wales presented at Caernafon
Edward III	1327–1377	Chaucer writes **Canterbury Tales**. Black Death (bubonic plague) Saw mill invented in Europe
Henry IV	1399–1413	Trade Guilds began to be formed
Henry V	1413–1422	Battle of Agincourt
Henry VI	1422–1461	Eton College and Kings College Cambridge founded
Edward IV	1461–1483	Caxton starts printing in England
Richard III	1483–1485	In 1485 at the Battle of Bosworth, Henry Tudor, later known as Henry VII, ends the medieval period of British history when he allegedly finds the royal crown which had fallen off Richard's head, and places it on his own

LATE MIDDLE AGES
1350 – 1485

In the previous section, we looked at the furniture of the Middle Ages, and we continue in that vein here. *Fig 1.4a* shows a 14th-century manuscript depicting a writing desk, an X-frame chair, and a form of bookcase with both cupboards and drawers. The drawers are bottom-hung and have ring pulls. Although one can assume a certain amount of artistic licence, all the furniture shown in this room is balanced, well made and far from crude. Some writers indicate that furniture did not achieve any degree of sophistication until the 16th century; but evidence from contemporary manuscripts proves otherwise. Our ancestors in the 14th and 15th centuries were adept wood technicians and were capable of producing very stylish articles as well as robustly built vernacular furniture.

Some writers indicate that furniture did not achieve any degree of sophistication until the 16th century; but evidence from contemporary manuscripts proves otherwise

Above: Fig 1.4a **14th-century manuscript depicting a writing desk, an X-frame chair, and a form of bookcase with both cupboards and drawers.**

Bottom right: Fig 1.4b **Replica of a table in a reconstructed medieval building at The Weald and Downland Open Air Museum, Singleton, England.**

BOARD TABLES

The next illustration, *see Fig 1.4b*, shows a table set on two trestles and covered with a linen tablecloth on which are set wooden platters, and pewter, brass and pottery utensils.

Above: Fig 1.4c 'Board' table — also from The Weald and Downland Open Air Museum, England.

Right middle: Fig 1.4d A more sophisticated form of seating – stool from the 15th century.

Right bottom: Fig 1.4e Table dating from the 16th century – these small tables were a natural development of the monastic furniture of the 14th and 15th centuries.

This table is a modern replica in a reconstructed medieval building at The Weald and Downland Open Air Museum at Singleton in the south of England.

The second table, *see Fig 1.4c*, also at Singleton, is again of simple form. These tables are often referred to in contemporary writing as 'boards' for obvious reasons; these words are still retained in the language today – we often refer to 'boardrooms' and the person who sits at the head of the table is known as the 'chairman' – in the Middle Ages it was common for there to be only one chair at the head of the table – everyone else sat on benches. Note the simple seating – a bench and a stool.

A more complex stool from the 15th century is shown in *Fig 1.4d* showing the delicate Gothic tracery. This stool is in the Victoria and Albert Museum in London.

INFLUENCES

Another table is shown in *Fig 1.4e*. This is slightly later than our period as it dates from the 16th century but I have included it because the drawers are similar to those in *Fig 1.4a*, and I am sure that such small tables were a natural development of the monastic furniture of the 14th and 15th centuries.

Fig 1.4f on page 26 shows some simple medieval household furniture. The emphasis, in vernacular furniture at least, is on simplicity and ease of making – very similar to the Arts and Crafts Movement 500 years later – it was, of course, this 'rural idyll' that inspired the Movement.

" While 15th-century northern Europe was using carved decoration, Italy was quickly returning to a classical style "

Above: Fig 1.4f **Simple medieval household furniture – simplicity is the key here.**

Below left: Fig 1.4g **Illustration from a 15th-century manuscript depicting card players around a circular table.**

Below right: Fig 1.4h **Interior of a 15th-century continental stateroom – note the piece on the left of the dais which shows the origins of the 'cup-board'.**

CUPBOARDS

Fig 1.4h shows the interior of a 15th-century Continental stateroom. To the left of the dais is an amazing construction of receding tiers with assorted cups, flagons and other vessels on it. Pieces of this type are the origin of the 'cup-board'. A gift of a twelve-step buffet from France to Henry VIII is recorded. These pieces of display furniture – land was less ravaged by wars, and it was safe to display valuables instead of locking them away – were soon perceived to be too big and heavy. The result was smaller, but more ornate, buffets or plate cupboards. An example, taken from a French manuscript is shown in *Fig 1.4j*.

One of the popular entertainments of medieval England was card playing. *Fig 1.4g* is taken from a 15th century manuscript which illustrates this pastime taking place on a circular table – which looks much like a 'Victorian Gothic Revival' piece.

DEVELOPMENTS

Two important developments occurred in the Middle Ages. The first was that of linenfold panelling, introduced to Britain by Flemish craftsmen in the 14th and 15th centuries. The second was the invention of the water-powered saw mill in the early 14th century in Germany. The introduction of the saw mill to this country was resisted for many years by the pit sawyers, so Continental furniture enjoyed an advantage over British furniture. However, the conversion of timber by hand had no deleterious effect on the quality of British cabinetmaking.

EUROPE

While 15th-century northern Europe was using carved decoration, Italy was quickly returning to a classical style. Inlay in coloured woods for some splendid architectural marquetry was becoming very fashionable. *Fig 1.4i* shows an example from the sacristy of Florence Cathedral. It is often thought that marquetry was developed in the 17th century; this is not so – in fact the Italians were developing the techniques as early as the 14th century.

TIMBERS

The list of timbers used by medieval craftsmen is given by Chaucer in 'The Parlement of Foules' and includes oak, elm, ash, holm oak, fir, box, cypress, yew, olive, laurel, poplar, willow, plane, hazel, chestnut, lime, maple and thorn.

This is an extensive list, and the diversity of timbers used is further evidence of the considerable understanding that medieval craftsmen had of their subject. Notwithstanding this, the major components of decoration in a medieval

Above: Fig 1.4j **A further development of the 'cup-board' depicted in a French manuscript.**

Above left: Fig 1.4i **Detail from the sacristy of Florence Cathedral demonstrates the fashion for inlay in intarsia and marquetry.**

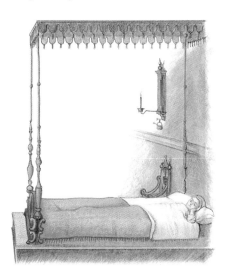

Above: Fig 1.4k **Reproduction of a picture painted in 1495 by Italian artist, Carpaccio.**

room were the fabrics used, not the items of furniture. This may date from the time when everyone moved around from castle to castle and took their richly decorated fabrics with them folded into baggage and carried on pack horses and wagons. The derivation of the French word for furniture, *meubles*, is from the word for 'moveables' – that which you take with you.

SOPHISTICATION

Fig 1.4k is a reproduction of a picture painted in 1495 by an Italian artist, Carpaccio. This shows a bedroom in an Italian mansion – I think that the furniture speaks for itself. Again we must allow for artistic licence, but note the delicacy of the lamp bracket hanging on the wall to the right of the bed. Bearing in mind that most of the objects depicted in the room were made in the last quarter of the 15th century; the room looks comfortable enough to spend a holiday in today.

RENAISSANCE
1460 – 1600

We have now reached the point in time when more obvious national styles developed. The 'Renaissance', meaning 're-birth', was an intellectual and artistic movement that started in the numerous Ducal courts of the area that was to become, in the 19th century, the modern state of Italy. The spread of ideas among writers and artists in the late 15th century soon crossed national boundaries and gave rise to Renaissance furniture and decorations throughout Europe.

Above: Fig 1.5a **16th-century walnut cupboard.**

Below: Photo 1.5b **16th-century table carved with the family arms of Pope Pius III.**

ITALIAN RENAISSANCE

Italian Renaissance furniture has a combination of restrained classical Greek and Roman design blended together with refined Byzantine high-relief ornament. The decorations on the objects are restrained in comparison with today's impression of the 'great' periods of Continental furniture such as those of Louis XlV to Louis XVl.

Fig 1.5a shows a 16th-century walnut cupboard, 4ft 8in high by 6ft 2in wide (1422mm high by 1880mm wide).This was sold at Sotheby's in London and was on view, giving everyone a chance to see a piece of furniture 500 years old.

Fig 1.5b shows a table of the same date which was also on view in London. It is carved with the arms of the family of Pope Pius lll (1439–1503) who almost certainly commissioned the table to be made. Although there are carved scrolled supports, they are not as 'over the top' as much 18th-century decoration was.

Another Italian piece is shown in *Fig 1.5c*. It is a walnut cassone or chest, 5ft 8in long and 2ft high (1728mm long by 610mm high). Again it is carved with the arms of the commissioning family – Guicciardini of Florence – and decorated in mathematical precision with beads, strapwork, fish scales, gadrooning and fluting.

" *The spread of ideas among writers and artists in the late 15th century soon crossed national boundaries and gave rise to Renaissance furniture and decorations throughout Europe* "

Above: Fig 1.5c **Walnut cassone or chest carved with the arms of the commissioning family – Guicciardini of Florence – and decorated in mathematical precision with beads, strapwork, fish scales, gadrooning and fluting.**

Right: Fig 1.5d **From an engraving by Dürer entitled 'St Jerome in his Study' – the table has 'slab' ends, their solidity relieved by an early form of cabriole support, and wedged rails.**

EARLY 16TH CENTURY

Fig 1.5d is taken from 'St Jerome in his Study', an engraving by Dürer dated 1515. The table is of familiar construction with 'slab' ends, their solidity relieved by an early form of cabriole support, and wedged stretchers. There is a bench around the room, reminiscent of the built-in furniture of the 13th and 14th centuries. There is a chair, with a cushion, for guests, which is very like that of the Arts and Crafts Movement. A small coffer sits under the bench, and hanging shelves carry candlesticks and writing implements.

ITALIAN STYLE

The table shown in *Fig 1.5e* on page 30 is quite different from that at which St Jerome is working. This is an Italian walnut centre table raised on dolphin supports. It measures 7ft by 2ft 6in (2134 by 762mm). The difference in outlook between northern and southern Europe is demonstrated by the differences in decoration between these two tables. The northern table is austere and simple while the Italian table is based on classical proportions with repetitive geometric mouldings, and has romanticized dolphin supports.

EXCEPTIONS

There are of course exceptions to any generalization. The Italian panel in *Fig 1.5f* on page 30 measures 18ft 3in by 6ft 3in (5580mm by 1930mm) and dates from the end of the 15th century. The monks on the right are shown in simple surroundings and the decorative panel on the left is gracefully simple with no trace of over decoration.

COLLECTORS' CABINET

A French cabinet dating from the early 16th century is shown in *Fig 1.5g*. It is made of walnut and measures 5ft high by 3ft 7in wide (1524mm high by 1093mm wide). The carved upper doors opened to reveal twelve small drawers. These cabinets were known as collectors' cabinets because the drawers were often used to contain small souvenirs and curios collected on travels.

HAND WARMER

The Spanish carved circular dish shown in *Fig 1.5i* has a copper brazier in the centre which would have been filled with charcoal, placed on a small stand and used on a table as a hand warmer. I include it because of the wonderful carved border in which the mythological creatures are designed to fill the space available, but do so in an elegant and balanced way.

HOUSEHOLD FURNITURE

Fig 1.5h shows another engraving by Dürer dating from the beginning of the 16th century. This is entitled 'The Birth of Mary'. The curtained bed is the forerunner of our four-poster bed. The other furniture consists of no less than three coffers with rising lids for storing linen, a table with slab ends, stools, shelves, a towel rail and a staved bucket for washing the baby in – all simple items, both recognizable and easily made nowadays with no mystery of the 'antique' about them, even though they were in use 500 years ago.

Top: Fig 1.5e **Italian walnut centre table on dolphin supports.**

Right: Fig 1.5f **Italian panel dating from the end of the 15th century.**

Above: Fig 1.5g **Collectors' cabinet in walnut.**

Right: Fig 1.5h **From an engraving by Dürer entitled 'The Birth of Mary' – the furniture is simple and could easily be made today.**

Above: Fig 1.5i **Spanish carved circular dish with a copper brazier in the centre – used as a hand warmer on cold winter nights.**

RELEVANT DATES

1460–1600	Renaissance
1485–1603	Tudor Kings and Queens
1445–1510	Botticelli
1452–1519	Leonardo da Vinci
1475–1564	Michelangelo
1483–1520	Raphael
1469–1527	Machiavelli
1451–1506	Columbus
1466–1536	Erasmus, Father of the Reformation of the Churches in Europe
1480–1530	Printed books became more easily available

TUDOR 1485 – 1603

The Tudor period is often thought of as England's 'Golden Age'. Henry VIII and Elizabeth I were monarchs, Shakespeare wrote play masterpieces and the English Navy built and sailed wonderful oak ships. In fact oak was a major material of the time – defences, houses, and furniture were all made of it.

The popular impression of Tudor furniture is of heavy sideboards, joint stools, refectory tables and the Great Bed of Ware. In this instance that impression is accurate!

Left: Fig 1.6a **Elizabethan oak court-cupboard.**
Below: Fig 1.6b **Elizabethan draw-leaf table in oak.**

PERIOD OF STABILITY

With the end of the Wars of the Roses in 1485, England entered a more stable period of history. All the non-military arts and activities flourished. Furniture-makers were able to consider comfort and ornament as well as robust functionality – settees and dining tables were for people who had leisure time.

English carvers had a strong design tradition that was based more on shapes taken from plants and animals than from the classical world. This was the time in furniture history when makers began to take design seriously and produce objects that were balanced and complete in themselves. The English oak court-cupboard in *Fig 1.6a* is a good example of this – its proportions are elegant and fulfilling, leaving the eye satisfied.

Fig 1.6b shows an Elizabethan oak draw-leaf table. I am sure that everyone is familiar with the idea of a double top-surface made of planks – the lower planks pull out to form an extension, held in place by the weight of the upper planks. Note the massive baluster turnings with carved decoration and the carving on the underside of the frieze.

Above: Fig 1.6c **Chair dating from about 1580 – it has a solid back above a seat that looks remarkably like a 'joint stool'.**

Right: Fig 1.6d **Solid-framed chair with a box or cupboard below.**

REFINEMENTS

Craft techniques were also being refined. The differences between carpenters and joyners had been defined in previous centuries. Carpenters no longer made furniture, except perhaps in the provinces which always lagged twenty or thirty years behind London. Joyner-cabinetmakers were looking for lighter, more elegant ways of making and decorating their furniture – the term cabinetmaker had not really been coined at this stage, but the embryo was there. On the other side of the channel, the ébénistes in France were about to become a distinct grouping and the Huguenots in the Low Countries were producing craftsmanship that produced specialist divisions of labour and skills. There was considerable interchange of ideas between mainland Europe and England and the skilled guilds were anxious to keep up with their European contemporaries.

Above: Fig 1.6e **Carpentry tools from a cabin on the** Mary Rose. **Copyright: Mary Rose Trust**

SEATING

Seating in the non-aristocratic houses still took the form of stools and benches. This continued until after the Civil War period when caned chairs introduced by William and Mary became more common. The chair in *Fig 1.6c* on page 33, which dates from about 1580, has a solid back above a seat that looks remarkably like a 'joint stool'. In fact, this was exactly how the chair developed – the rear legs of the stool were extended to form a back, the front legs raised to form arm-rests – and the basic design for the next 500 years had appeared.

There is a wide range of chairs and it is not possible to show them all. *Fig 1.6d* on page 33 depicts a solid-framed chair with a box or cupboard below, sometimes ascribed to the north of England; and *Fig 1.6f*, shows a 'turner's chair' made in yew wood. I must admit that I find it hard to accept that these latter chairs were comfortable, but so many were made that there was obviously a market for them.

THE REAL THING

Fig 1.6g is of another refectory table. It is a later piece, dating from the second quarter of the 17th century, but if it is not included here it will probably be pushed to one side by more exotic pieces of Jacobean and early Stuart art. It is

Above: Fig 1.6f **Early 17th-century turned armchair in yew wood with bobbin and spindle turnings and solid oak triangular seat.**

Right: Fig 1.6g **Oak refectory table, dated 1637.**

BRIDGING THE GAP

For a moment let us go back to the late 15th century or early 16th century to consider a piece of furniture that bridges the gap between Gothic and Tudor. *Fig 1.6h* shows a replica of an original piece of furniture that is in the Victoria and Albert Museum, London. This piece is so well known that it has a name – the Prince Arthur cupboard. It is an aumbry, a cupboard probably used for storing food. The cupboard was made in this century to the proportions of, and inspired by, the design of the original in the Victoria and Albert Museum. The top door appears to have the letter 'A', and the lower doors have feathers – both forming the pierced design.

Whether made for Prince Arthur or not, the original is certainly one of the earliest pieces of Tudor furniture extant, and shows the way in which Gothic designs ran on into the Tudor period. This of course is not uncommon, the division of time into historic periods is of benefit only to the historian who likes to put labels on objects – the craftsmen made what the client was going to pay for, whether it was twenty years out of date or twenty years before its time.

Above: Fig 1.6h **A replica of the Prince Arthur cupboard – the original can be viewed in the Victoria and Albert Museum, London.**

WEALD AND DOWNLAND OPEN AIR MUSEUM

These room settings at the Weald and Downland Open Air Museum in the south of England show furniture made in the last twenty years to designs that were prevalent in the 16th and 17th centuries. The furniture found in the houses of yeomen, merchants and smallholders was much simpler than that produced for centres of fashion. It might take a hundred years for styles to change so the images shown here are appropriate to both the buildings and the period. It is likely though that there would have been fewer items in the average early Tudor bedroom than in the average late Stuart bedroom.

dated 1637 and although there are some restorations, the majority of the structure is of the period. This table was sold for £15,000 (US$26,000) at Sotheby's in England in 1998. The viewing days were open to all, and any woodworker who wanted to see and touch objects made 450 years ago was free to examine the table. There is no excuse for saying that antiques are not accessible to non-collectors – so get into the salerooms on your hands and knees with a torch and notebook to study some heritage!

TUDOR FURNITURE ON SHOW

Many country houses have good collections of Tudor furniture. Knole House in Kent, England is one. Knole has given its name to this type of settee with sides and back joined by heavy knotted tassels.

RELEVANT DATES

1485	Henry Tudor defeats Richard III at the Battle of Bosworth Field to become the first Tudor monarch
1509	Henry VIII ascends the throne
1545	**Mary Rose** ship sinks
1547	Edward VI ascends the throne – he founds a number of grammar schools throughout England
1549	Book of Common Prayer
1553	Mary ascends the throne
1558	Elizabeth I ascends the throne
1564	William Shakespeare born
1588	Spanish Armada defeated – mostly due to bad weather
1598	Globe Theatre built in London using reclaimed oak due to high cost of timber
1603	James Stuart VI King of Scotland becomes James I of England

17TH CENTURY PART I
EUROPEAN FURNITURE

In the 17th century there were huge developments in exploration, science and the arts. There were still wars going on in Europe, but the aristocrats and the merchants wanted to flaunt their taste and wealth. Decoration on furniture became as important as function and, consequently, design boundaries were pushed out, with all manner of materials being used. The frequent religious wars in Europe meant that the craftsmen, many of whom were Protestant, fled to liberal countries such as England and the Netherlands.

Above: Fig 1.7a **Marquetry cabinet in the manner of Pierre Gole from the middle of the 17th century.**

Below: Fig 1.7b **A mid 17th-century Dutch cabinet with painted panels – the stand is a later addition.**

EBONIZING AND LACQUERING

Fig 1.7b, on the right, is of a mid 17th-century Dutch cabinet, 32in wide and 26in high, seen here on a later stand. This sort of cabinet was made to be placed on a table and left open to show off the painted panels. Famous artists of the time painted panels on copper specifically to be used in furniture.

The scenes on the cabinet are biblical, but set in contemporary landscapes. The surfaces around the panels are ebonized, which is not to be confused with lacquering. Ebonizing is a technique which attempts to make a piece of plain timber appear to be ebony – a very precious and valuable material. The process of ebonizing is essentially that of using a stain contained in a varnish or polish. Lacquer, be it the European imitation called 'Japanning' or real Oriental lacquer, is a form of decoration in itself – it is not trying to be something else. Lacquer may be black, red, green or multi-coloured.

The other decoration on this cabinet is oil-gilding. This is the laying of gold leaf on the wood using gold-size, which is a form of varnish. The process of gilding is several thousand years old.

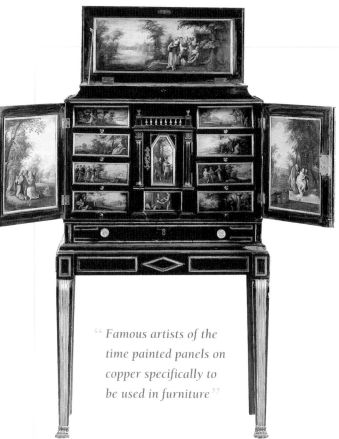

" *Famous artists of the time painted panels on copper specifically to be used in furniture* "

Above: Fig 1.7c **Table cabinet veneered in ebony and inlaid with ivory.**

MARQUETRY WORK

Fig 1.7a shows a marquetry cabinet in the manner of Pierre Gole, of Paris, who was born 1620 and died in 1684. Instead of the panels being painted, they have been inlaid in marquetry in the style of an artist called Monnoyer who died in 1699.

The cabinet is 54in wide and 27in high. The stand has been added later and is ebonized. The central door opens to reveal a marquetry perspective view of an architectural interior concealing mirrors and hidden drawers.

In Fig 1.7c we see another table cabinet, 24in wide. This is veneered in ebony and inlaid with ivory. The hemi-spherical domed architectural interior contains a series of small compartments and drawers.

TURNING AND CARVING

The next two illustrations, *see Figs 1.7d and 1.7e*, are of floor-standing cabinets, neither of which have inlaid or applied surfaces. *Fig 1.7d* shows an Italian walnut cabinet with lozenge panels and turned columns. The cabinet in *Fig 1.7e* which has low relief carving on the doors is also made from walnut, but is French in origin. These two cabinets illustrate the difference between Italian and French design – Italian design was austere and simple, whereas French designs were gentler and more naturalistic, even though the columns in the Northern European example are from the Corinthian Order which has its origins on the Mediterranean coast. The French cabinet is standing on 'bun' feet which were added later. There are two main reasons for later feet – one is that the originals may have rotted because of the damp floors on which the furniture stood, or the misuse of the cleaner's mop and bucket! The other possible reason is that when members of a family inherited their ancestors' furniture

"The process of gilding is several thousand years old"

they very often tried to make it look 'lighter' and more modern by raising it up, allowing more visible light to be seen underneath the object, and fitting feet or plinths that were fashionable at the time.

TABLES

Tables continued to be either simple for vernacular use, or heavy and ornate, *see Figs 1.7f and 1.7g*. Both designs were continuations of those produced in the previous century.

A new type of table was also being produced, *see Fig 1.7h*. This was really the start of a trend that was to continue until the present day – the 'specimen table'. Such tables were intended as 'show offs'. The example illustrated is made from ebony and ivory and is dated circa 1600, and was probably

Above: Fig 1.7f **From a painting by Daniele Crespi, dated 1625, showing an 'ordinary' early 17th-century Italian interior.**

Left: Fig 1.7g **Centre table of carved walnut, dated 1630, made in Piedmont.**

made in Florence. Note that the edges of the octagon have been rubbed through and have been made out of pale coloured wood that has been ebonized. These lippings were too long to produce in ebony – or they may have been lost.

A similar table is recorded as being in the collection of The Duke of Norfolk at Arundel Castle, England which is open to the public. Other forms of specimen tables include the pietre-dure – which is marquetry in coloured stones – along with tables made entirely in marble or those produced with unusual timbers.

ORIENTAL LACQUER

Oriental lacquer is made by applying a recipe which contains sap from the Rhus tree – sometimes known as the 'lacquer tree' – to wooden surfaces. The process is repeated many times and rubbed down between each coat. The resultant surfaces, after curing, are durable, capable of taking a high shine, and will resist boiling water and acids.

Lacquer objects over 1000 years old have been found in China and Japan. For further study find a copy of *Lacquer: an International History and Collector's Guide*, Crowood Press, Marlborough, 1984.

Fig 1.7h **'Specimen table' made from ebony and ivory and dated circa 1600.**

The publication of the classical orders of column parts led to the use of such designs in furniture, architecture and the decorative arts.

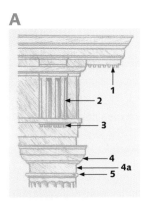

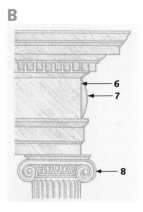

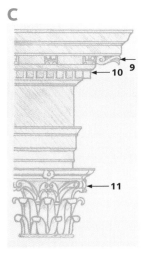

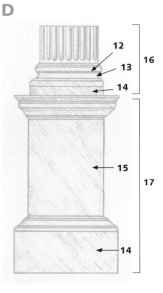

A THE DORIC ORDER

1 Mutule
2 Triglyph
3 Guttae
4 Necking (Trachelion)
4a Hypotrachelion
5 Astragal

B THE IONIC ORDER

6 Flat frieze
7 Pulvinated (Convex) frieze
8 Volutes, diagonally placed

C THE CORINTHIAN ORDER

9 Modillion
10 Dentils
11 Acanthus foliage in outline showing its arrangement round the bell

D PEDESTAL

12 Torus
13 Scotia
14 Plinth
15 Die/Dado
16 Base
17 Pedestal (Attic base)

MIRRORS

Mention must be made of another object that began to appear this century – the mirror. The example shown here, *see Fig 1.7i*, dates from the mid 17th century and has replacement glass. The subject of mirror glass would fill an article in itself, so I will refer you to a superb book on the subject – *World Mirrors* by G. Child, published by Sotheby's. Our example has an oil-gilded frame which was carved, and then had gesso, made of whiting and rabbit glue, applied – this in turn was carved, giving a very crisp and finely detailed surface onto which the beaten gold leaf could be applied.

Above: Fig 1.7i **A mid 17th-century mirror with replacement glass and an oil-gilded frame.**

RELEVANT DATES

1610	Louis XIII ascends the French throne
1624	Cardinal Richelieu becomes First Minister in France
1626	Dutch explorers found New York
1627	Siege of La Rochelle (**Three Musketeers** by Alexandre Dumas set in this period)
1642	First sightings of Australasia by Dutch navigators
1643	Louis XIV King of France, Cardinal Mazarin Chief Minister
1648	End of Thirty Years' War, Dutch Republic recognised as Independent
1665–74	Various wars between France and England and the Netherlands
1674	Treaty of Westminster between England and the Netherlands
1677	William III of the Netherlands marries Mary, heir to English throne
1682	French Court installed at Versailles
1683	Siege of Vienna by Ottoman Empire
1685	Edict of Nantes revoked in France Protestantism forbidden 50,000 Huguenot families leave France with many craftsmen amongst them
1697	Treaty of Ryswick between France, England, Spain and Netherlands Ottoman Empire defeated at Battle of Zenta

17TH CENTURY PART II
ÉBÉNISTES

France was the first country to really create a national style of furniture. The position of the French monarchy and aristocracy allowed them to indulge in major patronage of all the arts, including that of cabinetmaking. French cabinetmakers were known as ébénistes, that is 'those that work in ebony'. Not all furniture was made in ebony, nor did the ébénistes confine themselves to the use of that timber. The name ébéniste simply came about because at the time that the designer/makers became well known, the fashion was for furniture which was decorated with ebony.

BAROQUE

The main design style of the 17th century was Baroque. This was a voluptuous, curvaceous style in which everything was slightly 'over the top'. Indeed, many pieces of furniture were over-decorated with massive ornaments and enormous pediments. Gone were the days of classical restraint.

ANDRÉ-CHARLES BOULLE

Probably the most famous ébéniste was André-Charles Boulle (1642–1732). He was the inventor of the process which bears his name – that of inlaying brass in tortoiseshell.

Sometimes other materials were used such as pewter and, in exceptional pieces, the inlays were mirror images of each other. This was called '*boulle*' and '*contre-boulle*'. Such pieces were usually made in pairs.

ORMOLU

Fig 1.8a shows a copy of a bureau-plat made at the end of the 17th, or the start of the 18th century, in Boulle's workshop. The period in which Boulle was most prolific spans the two centuries. French desks were more often than not flat writing tables, which is just about what bureau-plat means. This table is decorated with gilt mounts which are sometimes known as '*ormolu*'. The name is derived from the

Above: Fig 1.8a **Bureau-plat in the style made famous by André-Charles Boulle.**

Below: Fig 1.8b **Detail of boulle-work – all the material in this panel is hand-cut, and the shapes are taken from pattern books containing engravings which were fashionable at the time.**

Above: Fig 1.8c **Design drawn by Boulle in 1701.**

Right: Fig 1.8d **Armoire based on this design.**

French for gold, and molu, meaning 'mashed'. The mounts were made from brass that had been covered in 'mashed up gold'. In fact, the technique involved mixing gold with mercury paste – hence the 'mash' – applying the paste to the brass mount, heating the whole thing up so that the mercury vapourized, which left behind the gold which was fused to the brass substrate. The technique is also known as 'fire-gilding' and, because of the use of mercury, is now banned without very expensive health and safety precautions.

BOULLE-WORK

Fig 1.8b shows a detail of boulle-work – all the material in this panel is hand-cut, and the shapes are taken from pattern books containing engravings which were fashionable at the time.

For interest, I show a design drawn by Boulle in 1701, together with an armoire that was based on this design, *see Figs 1.8c and 1.8d.*

MARQUETRY

I find it quite remarkable that marquetry work of great finesse could be undertaken 300 years ago, without any artificial light and very few books. In 1715 Boulle was known to have in his workshop about 250 sketches and studies of birds and flowers, and an inventory taken at the time lists some of the timbers he used – bois jaune, ash, bois rouge known as sandalwood, stetin, box, thorn, barberry, holly, Brazil, and others.

MAKING IT PAY

Although this was a 'golden age' for the making of furniture, an intriguing quotation about the hierarchy within the trade from a French commentator, Roubo, is as applicable today as it was in the 17th century "…most of them (the ébénistes) work exclusively for the merchants who do not pay what the work is worth. The luxury in fashion today is also one of the causes of the lack of finish in ébénisterie, as everyone wishes to own it (fine furniture) without having the means to pay for its true value. The ébénistes do not make the carcasses themselves but have them made at rock-bottom prices by other cabinet-makers who do nothing but make carcasses." This might account for the curious fact, noted by many restorers, that the carcass-work of Continental furniture is diabolical, while the visible surfaces are stunning.

MAZARIN

Another form of bureau is the Mazarin shown in *Fig 1.8e*. It is named after the Chief Minister of Louis XIV. A desk of this form is known to have been delivered to the French Court in 1669. By the last quarter of the 17th century this form of desk was extremely popular. However, the bureau-plat superseded it, and remains a popular form of desk today.

EVERYDAY FURNITURE

Not all furniture was made for sovereigns and aristocrats. *Fig 1.8f* shows a little drop-leaf centre table veneered in boxwood and amboyna. The turned legs and stretcher are much more familiar than the gilded pieces shown earlier. This type of table was found both on the Continent and in Britain.

CACHE-POTS

Fig 1.8h, is of a beautiful cache-pot – a little plant holder. The flower-pot is put inside the boulle container. It is made of gilt-brass and tortoiseshell with a white metal liner.

ARMOIRE

My final illustration, *Fig 1.8i* shows a tortoiseshell and ebony armoire with glazed doors. This is a simpler piece, without the brass inlay and probably used as a bookcase, although here the shelves are missing.

> " *The period in which Boulle was most prolific spans the two centuries* "

Above: Fig 1.8e **Marquetried top of a Mazarin bureau.**

Right: Fig 1.8f **Drop-leaf centre table veneered in boxwood and amboyna.**

ECOLE BOULLE

The École Boulle (*Fig 1.8g*) is based in Paris and is a state-run school for ébénistes where students train for up to seven years, achieving some of the very finest work. The school is named after André-Charles Boulle.

Students either enter the school at a more advanced level and do a five-year ébéniste course, or they join at an intermediate level and follow a seven-year course, which includes a certain amount of academic study. There are over 1,000 students at the school in total.

Right: Fig 1.8g **The École Boulle, Paris – a state-run school for ébénistes.**

" Consider making any one of these pieces with hand tools, no electric light, without the use of a telephone, camera or delivery van, and you can see the quantum jump in skills from the 16th century to the 17th century "

DESIGNER OBJECTS

Consider making any one of these pieces with hand tools, no electric light, without the use of a telephone, camera or delivery van, and you can see the quantum jump in skills from the 16th century to the 17th century.

In these short articles it is impossible to do justice to the importance of the ébénistes who were the first cabinetmakers to be accepted into high society. In a sense, the culture of 'designer objects' which is prevalent today began with the ébénistes in the 17th century.

" Boulle was known to have in his workshop about 250 sketches and studies of birds and flowers "

Left: Fig 1.8h **A cache-pot or plant-holder made of gilt-brass and tortoiseshell with white-metal liner.**

Above: Fig 1.8i **Tortoiseshell and ebony armoire with glazed doors.**

17TH CENTURY PART III
CHAIRS

Although there was considerable fighting in the 17th century there was a general growth in luxury items, whether it be exotic spices from the mysterious East or simply the provision of comfortable seating. In this survey of furniture the chair has, until this section, been considered as part of the general grouping 'furniture'. From now on, the chair becomes one of the most important articles in that grouping and will merit detailed description.

Left: Fig 1.9a **Italian walnut chair from the beginning of the 17th century – comfort is not high on the list here.**

CHAIRS

Chairs are one of the most abused categories of furniture. The simple 20th-century chair on which I am sitting, as I write, has 28 joints in it. The man who made it had the advantage of machines with repeat settings and as much light as he wanted. To make a chair that can carry the weight of a heavy person and last for 350 years required much skill and many experiments. However, the basic design of chairs was formalized in the 17th century and lasts until the present day.

ABUSE

I mentioned that the chair was abused. The design that the 17th-century makers evolved withstands dragging, rocking, twisting and being used as a pair of steps. Of course such abuse does eventually take its toll and a visit to the restorer is needed. What happens? The owner will not spend the money on repair, but leaves the chair in a corner or a spare bedroom with weakened joints until it finally collapses. Thus the poor chair has been the victim of abuse and neglect.

TIMBERS

The first illustration, *see Fig 1.9a*, shows an Italian walnut chair dating from the beginning of the 17th century. The timbers are still square in section, heavy and without much consideration for comfort. The fabric has been replaced but the close nailing is as might have been undertaken originally.

The next examples, *see Fig 1.9b*, are again in walnut, but French, dating from the first half of the 17th century. The general structure is still rectangular, but the heavy lines of square-section timbers are replaced with bobbin turning. Such turning gave a lightness to the timbers but left the square sections at the joints, where the major stresses would be encountered.

Above: Fig 1.9b **Pair of French chairs in walnut dating from the first half of the 17th century incorporates turning to lighten the look.**

Above right: Fig 1.9c **This type of stool was being made in Europe from the latter part of the 16th century to the present day.**

Below: Fig 1.9d **Franco-Flemish chair, again in walnut, from the middle of the century makes some concessions towards comfort.**

COMFORT

Fig 1.9d, shows a Franco-Flemish chair, again in walnut, from the middle of the century. This time there are some concessions towards comfort. The back has a decent rake to it, the arms lending support to the back uprights. Back and arms are upholstered and a loose squab cushion is supplied. The upholstery has been replaced but the fringes are acceptable in terms of historic design.

THE STOOL

The stool shown in *Fig 1.9c*, is walnut and of standard joint-stool construction. Such stools were being made throughout Europe from the latter part of the 16th century to the present day. The cushion is possibly a later addition, but these stools would have been used with similar cushions in the 17th century.

ORNAMENT

The Tuscan chair with red damask upholstery, *see Fig 1.9f on page 46*, has unusual gilded finials and dates from the third quarter of the 17th century. Such ornamentation is a hangover from earlier centuries when only important people, who liked to be surrounded by badges and heraldic devices, had chairs. These finials are formed of entwined acanthus leaves, an ornament that was to become very popular in the 18th century. The chair still has square section members with only a small amount of turning. Turning was expensive and this designer was frugal.

LEATHER WORK

Fig 1.9e, shows a typical Iberian chair upholstered in embossed leather. The leather workers of the Spanish/ Portuguese peninsular had become famous by the 17th century, as they still are, and although it looks rather delicate, such chairs, when properly glued up – the joints almost always work loose – are quite comfortable.

SETTEE

A 17th-century settee is shown in *Fig 1.9h*. Chairmakers had now become confident enough to make 'double chairs' which were the forerunners of today's settee. The main members of this late 17th-century French settee are similar in section to those of the chairs shown above, but extended to form a wide seat. Previously, if two people were to sit side by side, they would have had to have done so on a solid bench. The central leg supports the seat rails which are usually thickened up for obvious reasons.

As an aside it is worth mentioning that settees are often altered either by having their rails cut or spliced and sometimes by being totally 'made up' out of a single chair. For this, the legs and sides are used and the long rails freshly made, or the original rails spliced.

Right: Fig 1.9h **17th-century French settee.**

" Such turning gave a lightness to the timbers but left the square sections at the joints, where the major stresses would be encountered "

Above: Fig 1.9i **Pair of stools of an earlier X-frame design but with curved legs.**

Above Right: Fig 1.9j **Pair of Régence armchairs whose arms, rails and legs are all curves.**

VERNACULAR CHAIR

Before we move into the last part of the 17th century and into a new design age, I show a set of ordinary vernacular chairs, upholstered in plain red velvet with simple solid turned legs and stretchers, *see Fig 1.9j*.

ARTISTIC STYLES

Unfortunately, artistic styles do not coincide exactly with the centuries. The end of the 17th century and the beginning of the 18th century were known in France as the 'Régence'. The stiff formality of the earlier years began to give way to softer more flowing lines.

My final four illustrations show this development, leaving the way clear in following articles to concentrate on the 18th century proper. *Fig 1.9k* shows a French gilded chair. Note the increase in carved decoration and particularly the languorous arms requiring some understanding of grain direction in relation to jointing and stresses.

DEVELOPMENTS

The next illustration, *Fig 1.9l*, shows a stool, quite unlike that shown in *Fig 1.9c* on page 45. The basic shape is still rectangular – but not for long – however, the surfaces are almost cluttered with decoration. The pair of stools shown next, *see Fig 1.9i*, although of an earlier X-frame design, have curvaceous members.

Finally we move into the first quarter of the 18th century with the pair of Régence armchairs whose arms, rails, and legs are all curves, *see Fig 1.9j*. In the space of two generations, chairmakers moved from straight timbers to flowing curves and complicated geometry. From what was a simple 'stool with a back' at the beginning of the 17th century, the exquisite art of chair-making had been born.

Far left: Fig 1.9k **French gilded chair from the latter part of the 17th century – note how the formality of the earlier era has become more soft and fluid.**

Left: Fig 1.9l **Although the basic shape of the stool remains the same, it has now become highly ornamented.**

When Queen Elizabeth I died in 1603, James VI of Scotland became James I of England – and thus the Scottish and English crowns were united. The 17th century is a complex period in political history, and a book that deals primarily with furniture is not an appropriate place to discuss it – but the furniture student does need to be aware of the Civil War and the place of William of Orange in British social history.

One might think that a time of civil war and an uncertain royal succession would result in a reduction of new design and styles, and to some extent this is true. The 'Protectorate' period during which Cromwell ruled the country resulted in much Puritan activity – rich furniture, carvings and ornamentation were destroyed and replaced with those displaying Puritan simplicity. In the period leading up to the Civil War (1639–49) many of the treasures of large country houses were destroyed or hidden away. However, in the early Stuart period (1603–1649) there was much interchange with Europe and the adoption of European styles of decoration. Again, in the latter part of the 17th century, when Parliament invited the Dutch prince, William of Orange, to rule England and Scotland, a new design ethos crept into our furniture-making.

Above: Fig 1.10a **Oak table dating from the reign of Charles I.**

Below: Fig 1.10b **Gateleg table in walnut – a new look for the Elizabethans.**

DINING TABLE

My first illustration shows a table dating from the reign of Charles I (1625–1649), *see Fig 1.10a*. It is in oak, as was most furniture at this time, and still has the general shape of a 'refectory table', so named from the refectories in which medieval monks took their meals. The joints are stout mortise and tenon and are pegged. This table would not have appeared particularly unusual to diners coming from the previous century

However, the next table shown, *see fig 1.10b*, which is familiar to us, would have appeared as rather new stylistically to the Elizabethans – it is a gateleg table in walnut. Gatelegs were known in the 16th century, but were not common. They reached their peak of production in the 100 years between the middle of the 17th and the middle of the 18th century. Big houses continued to have large formal dining tables, but lesser gentry and farmers began to furnish their smaller houses. They wanted a table that could be made larger for entertaining but which would fold away. The cottage dining table, as it later came to be known, was the answer. It is such an enduring style that they are still made today. If one thinks of an 'English' interior then a gateleg table, a dresser and an inglenook fireplace are what spring to mind.

Above: Fig 1.10c **Dresser dated 1696 – probably made as a wedding gift.**

Below: Fig 1.10d **Another form of dresser from the time of Charles II.**

DRESSERS

This brings us to the dresser. No one should talk about dressers without referring to Victor Chinnery's book, *Oak Furniture – The British Tradition.* My first example, *see Fig 1.10d*, dates from the time of Charles II (1660–1685). It has the basic shape of a coffer but instead of a hinged lid there is a row of drawers above two deeper drawers flanked by a pair of cupboards. Remember that the 14th-century origin of a dresser was a 'board for placing drinking cups on', so these 'cup boards' with doors large enough to insert big pieces of pewter-ware are the direct descendants of medieval tiered dressers. The whole piece is panelled within a mortise-and-tenoned frame. There is a loose equivalence between this frame-and-panel construction and bespoke kitchen

" *In the latter part of the 17th century, when Parliament invited the Dutch prince, William of Orange, to rule England and Scotland, a new design ethos crept into our furniture-making* "

'cup-boards' of today. Another form of dresser is shown in *Fig 1.10c*. This piece bears the date 1696 and the initials 'EHIR'. One should always be suspicious of dated pieces of furniture – Victorians loved putting spurious dates onto genuine but otherwise perfectly ordinary items. In this case the date and the initials form part of the panelling and the lettering is of such good quality that I believe they can be regarded as genuine. The piece was probably made as a wedding gift and the initials would be those of the bride and groom. Note the fact that the piece has a very late date, but is of an earlier, Elizabethan form. Many styles overlapped throughout the country and it is quite possible that this was made in the provinces to fit in with other late 16th- or early 17th-century furniture that the couple had inherited. The newfangled London, and even 'Dutch' styles, were disliked by the country patrons of the provincial joiner/cabinetmaker.

CLOCK CASE

My next illustration shows a clock case, *see Fig 1.10e*. This piece is unrestored so I apologize for the missing mouldings and broken feet. It shows the new style of inlay brought over from The Netherlands when Prince William and Queen Mary came to London. This style of marquetry is known as 'seaweed marquetry' and is, in English furniture, confined to the period from 1688, when William and Mary arrived, to the end of Anne's reign in 1714. Of course there was much exotic pictorial marquetry produced after this period, but the better work is associated with William and Mary. Purists will note that the plinth has been cut down, the lower border is missing, and swept bracket feet had not been invented!

Left: Fig 1.10e **Unrestored clock-case from the reign of William and Mary.**

Below: Fig 1.10f **Pair of chairs in oak with cane seats and backs.**

CHAIRS

Refectory tables could accommodate long benches for the diners, but oval gateleg tables needed standard chairs. I show two examples, both with cane panel backs. The earlier chairs of the century had solid backs, and indeed chairs with solid backs continued to be made well into the next century. The 17th century innovation in chair-making was the cane seat and back – it looked lighter and felt softer.

The pair of chairs, *see Fig 1.10f*, are from a set of six, made in oak, with a cane seat under the green squab cushions. Imagine how wonderful it must have felt to sit on these chairs after being brought up on hard benches and joint stools. This set is from the William and Mary period, while the armchair, *see Fig 1.10g*, is slightly earlier, Charles II, and is made from walnut. Again it has a caned seat. Both chairs have turned legs with square blocks at the joints. This is the last time we will see this construction because Georgian furniture uses much smaller section timbers.

" The 17th century innovation in chair-making was the cane seat and back – it looked lighter and felt softer "

Fig 1.10g **Walnut armchair from the Charles II period.**

CHEST

My final illustration, *see Fig 1.10h*, shows a late 17th-century chest. It is made of leather-covered deal and decorated with domed-head nails. This is another style of furniture which does not appear again. The coffer-maker went out of business at the end of the 17th century. Trunks with domed tops continued to be made, but after travelling they were unpacked and the contents put into chests-of-drawers. The coffer wasn't used for storage any more, except perhaps in an attic, it was used for travelling. So the elaborate craft of the cofferer, the decoration and elaboration of travelling boxes, much sought after in previous times, was no longer in demand.

Fig 1.10h **Late 17th-century chest.**

RELEVANT DATES

1603	James I crowned
1610	Louis XIII ascends the French throne
1611	Authorized version of the Bible completed – the so-called James I version
1625	Charles I crowned
1642	Civil War between Royalists (Cavaliers) and Parliamentarians (Roundheads)
1649	Charles I executed
1653	Cromwell becomes Lord Protector of England
1658	Cromwell dies
1660	Charles II restored to the throne of England and Scotland
1665	Newton discovers laws of gravity
1685	James II ascends throne
1689	William III ascends throne (William and Mary)
1702	Anne becomes Queen of England and Scotland

CHAPTER

TWO

The Age of Enlightenment

18TH-CENTURY ITALIAN FURNITURE

Furniture produced in the 18th century is considered to be the height of taste, design and construction. This is the case for pieces made for the upper end of the market, as indeed it is for all periods of history, but even the vernacular furniture has something special about it.

Because the period is so large, I will divide the furniture up by country of origin – this part deals with Italian furniture. It is sad to record that although Italian design and taste were very splendid, the construction of the furniture left a lot to be desired. Carcasses were made of badly seasoned timber, often poplar and fruitwoods, and the internal construction played a very definite second fiddle to the exterior appearance.

Left: Fig 2.1a **Venetian bureau-bookcase veneered in burr-walnut with parcel-gilt enrichments, made in the middle of the 18th century.**

Below: Fig 2.1b **Carved and gilded mirror with matching console table from Genoa.**

VENETIAN BOOKCASE

My first item, *see Fig 2.1a*, is a bureau-bookcase, 9ft 8in by 5ft 7in (2946mm high by 1700mm wide), veneered in burr-walnut with parcel-gilt enrichments. It was made in Venice in the middle of the 18th century. The general form of the piece is Anglo-Dutch and, as such, this type of bureau-bookcase has its origins in the association between England and Holland when William of Orange was offered the throne of England in 1689.

The gilding is only partial, and so referred to as 'parcel-gilt', the term coming from the idea that parcels were small things and there is only a small amount of gilding! The gilding is of the usual type, consisting of carved wood which is covered with a layer of gesso – a mix of chalk and glue which produces a smooth surface – onto which gold leaf is applied. I can hear gilders shout that is it not that simple but I am trying to avoid long footnotes and glossaries!

Fig 2.1c **Venetian console table with a faux-marble top above a giltwood base.**

THE BUREAU-BOOKCASE

The bureau-bookcase was intended to be one of the main eye-catching pieces of a reception room. The small piece of engraved mirror below the cresting is an example of the Venetian mirror makers' and engravers' art. The galleried interior would hold books as well as a few choice pieces of porcelain to enable the owner to display his taste and wealth, although it was not entirely a display piece as the fall would have been used for writing, and the drawers below are quite functional. The general shape is wavy, which is known as 'serpentine', and is a reaction to the straight lines of the previous century.

THE MIRROR

The other major item in a reception room was the mirror. The example shown here, *see Fig 2.1b*, is in the form of a mirror above a console table. Adorned with figures, masks and flowers, the whole group, made of carved and gilded wood, stands at an impressive 11ft (3352mm) high, and was made in Genoa in the second quarter of the century. It is more a sculpture than a piece of furniture, and shows the vast difference between Italian design concepts and those of Northern Europe. Whilst we have such carvings occurring in North Europe, they are more restrained and tighter than this flamboyant and loosely styled carving, so typical of Italian work.

GENOESE TABLE

The next example, *see Fig 2.1d*, is of another 'sculptural' piece, this time a table. Again it is from Genoa, made in the first half of the 18th century and veneered in tulipwood. The top is formed of a green marble veneer, set in a gilt bronze surround. Yes, you did read correctly – the marble is veneered. Much like timber, rare and precious marbles were cut into thin slices and glued onto cheaper and solid substrates.

Above: Fig 2.1d **Genoese table in veneered tulipwood – with a top that is veneered in green marble, set in a bronze surround.**

Centre: Fig 2.1e **Chest of drawers, or commode, from Naples in the second half of the 18th century.**

Bottom: Fig 2.1f **Commode veneered in palisander figuratively decorated with classically derived scenes.**

The base is mounted with carved dolphins, which is typical of items produced in an area that had a strong maritime tradition – indeed it was on that tradition that the wealth of the city was founded. The coat-of-arms is that of one of the Centurione of Genoa.

VENETIAN CONSOLE TABLE

Fig 2.1c, on page 55, shows another console table, this time Venetian, again of serpentine outline, with a faux marble top above a giltwood base. Again the maker has found a way of overcoming the scarcity of marble in his locality – the top has been painted to give the appearance of marble.

The quantity of carving and the depth of the frieze indicate a piece almost certainly designed for a grand interior.

NEAPOLITAN COMMODE

The next illustration, *see Fig 2.1e*, also on page 55, is of a much more modest chest of drawers, or commode, which comes from Naples and was made in the second half of the 18th century. It is of serpentine bombé form, has a solid marble top, and is veneered in kingwood and tulipwood.

The form, although still early 18th century, is slightly simpler than some of the previous items we have been looking at. The legs are intended to be thin and graceful but are a furniture remover's nightmare. This again is an example of form being more important than function.

The mounts are very dirty, but are of gilt bronze. Some collectors prefer such signs of age and would never want to have them cleaned. The 'dirt' is in fact tarnish which occurs at places where the gold has been worn away leaving the bronze/brass mixture underneath to react to airborne pollutants and human handling. This is often called 'patina'.

GRAND TOUR INFLUENCE

Now we move to the latter part of the 18th century. *Fig 2.1f*, on page 55, is of a commode veneered in palisander (rosewood) and is figuratively decorated with classically derived scenes. Gone are the strange legs and flowing decoration, to be replaced with elegance and simplicity. This piece was made in the time of 'The Grand Tour' when young men visited Italy to see the remains of Classical Rome and to bring home books of prints and drawings. The designs shown on these prints and drawings began to appear on furniture and interior decoration.

DECORATION

The next two examples, *see Figs 2.1g and 2.1h*, show forms of decoration that, although they appear elsewhere are best exemplified by the work of Italian craftsmen. *Fig 2.1g* shows a late 18th-century walnut marquetry penwork chest of drawers. Although contrasting veneers have been used to form the panelling and cartouches, the busts within the cartouches are engraved to simulate a penwork drawing. The line of the ink is made from black wax which is laid into the engraving prior to polishing – sometimes ink alone was used.

Above: Fig 2.1j **Italian bureau-bookcase dating from about 1730 and decorated with patriarchs, knights and chinoiserie scenes.**

Below: Fig 2.1k **Lacquered and parcel-gilt Venetian commode made in about 1740 – note how the handles, which are pendant fruits or nuts, form part of the design.**

Fig 2.1h shows a very pretty commode with painted decoration. In the damaged places one can see the gesso with which the piece has been covered in order to give a smooth ground for painting onto. Again the top is faux marble. Note the lack of handles – if the decorator felt that handles would spoil his design, he just removed them. The only way to open the drawers is by pulling on the key!

> " *It is more a sculpture than a piece of furniture, and shows the vast difference between Italian design concepts and those of Northern Europe* "

FRENCH INFLUENCE

Fig 2.1i shows an elegant pair of corner consoles dating from about 1780. Although these have some Italian classical decoration, such as the raised scrollwork within the frieze, they also show signs of French influence particularly in the legs.

Fig 2.1j shows a wonderful lacquered and parcel-gilt Venetian commode made in about 1740. Note that in this piece the handles, which are pendant fruits or nuts, form part of the design.

FALSE DRAWERS

We now come back to where we started, a bureau bookcase, *see Fig 2.1k*. Italian bureaux bookcases are so splendid that they deserve lots of space. This one dates from about 1730 and is decorated with patriarchs, knights and chinoiserie (imitation Chinese decorative objects) scenes.

The interior is subdivided in the same way that English bureaux bookcases of the same period are subdivided. Again the drawers have no handles. The first drawer under the fall has been altered – it is often the case that the first drawer is false, the space behind the drawer front being reached through a sliding well accessible from the interior of the writing compartment. This piece has been altered to allow a part of the first drawer to open.

The baskets of fruit on either side are later additions. The original drawer front has been cut down, and the fact that the horizontal gold line at the bottom of the first drawer only appears in the small opening section means that that part is original – the surround to the opening is a replacement and therefore none of the decoration matches up.

This gilding is not gold leaf, it is just gold paint, the reason for this being that the whole surface is intended to appear like Oriental lacquer.

18TH-CENTURY FRENCH
FURNITURE PART I

Fig 2.2a **Régence commode in Rio rosewood, made in about 1720. Rosewood was not extensively used in Britain until the end of the 18th century.**

Craftsmen and connoisseurs agree: French and English furniture of the 18th century is the finest ever made. With so many worthy items, it's hard to make a selection to discuss, and inevitable that some styles and examples will be left out. But let me start with a familiar term.

Even those who know little or nothing about French furniture, recognize the term 'Louis'. This misleading nomenclature came about because non-historians became bored with and confused by the stylistic differences between Louis XIV, XV, XVI, etc., and simply labelled French furniture as 'Louis'.

There is no such thing as a 'Louis' style. Each period had distinct differences and there was a logical progression between these design developments. In '17th Century, part II: Ébénistes' (pages 40–43), I described the curvaceous Baroque style of the 17th century. When Louis XIV died in 1715 massive changes occurred in French society and, as a consequence, also in furniture design and making.

ROSEWOOD

The new King, Louis XV, was just five years old and so a Regent was appointed. The first distinct period in the 18th century was known as Régence. Louis XV came of age in 1723 and the style named after him, 'Louis XV', lasted until the start of the Transitional period – *see date chart on page 61.*

The first illustration – *see Fig 2.2a* – shows a Régence commode in Rio rosewood (*Dalbergia nigra*). This commode was made in about 1720. The use of rosewood veneer on the Continent pre-dated its common usage in England by about 50 years.

The Régence style bridges the gap between the 'Sun King', Louis XIV and his great-grandson Louis XV; it is slightly restrained compared with the rococo style that came later in Louis XV's reign.

GROTTO

The next illustration – *see Fig 2.2b* – is of a full-blooded rococo commode made in the middle of the 18th century. The word 'rococo' is derived from the French for 'rock-work', and refers to the naturalistic grottoes and other hard landscape features in the Palace of Versailles.

Rococo was a sort of 'back to nature' style, in which the restraints of formalized design were discarded. The gilt metalwork on this commode is more flowing than that on the preceding item, although not as asymmetrical as art nouveau; some of the leaf scrolls look as though they were drawn from nature.

There is also more experimentation with the timbers. The piece is veneered in purpleheart (*Peltogyne pubescens*), bois satiné (Guiana/San Dominican mahogany), and bois-de-bout. It is stamped with the maker's name: J. Dubois (created Master Ébéniste in 1742).

Fig 2.2b **This commode from about 1750, in full rococo style, has leaf scrolls that might have been drawn from nature.**

" *This oriental form of decoration – raised giltwork on a black ground – was transposed on to the shapes of European furniture* "

PETALS

'Bois-de-bout' refers to the technique of cutting across the grain to give the marquetry flowers the appearance of petals seen on edge. The effect is particularly effective to the left-hand side of centre, above the apron.

The next illustration – *see Fig 2.2c* – shows a black japanned commode from the mid- to late-18th century. There was a sense of exploration at that time, as India and the Far East were opened up by trading companies. This oriental form of decoration – raised giltwork on a black ground – was transposed on to the shapes of European furniture. This two-drawer commode is a modest example, aimed to suit the middle-class merchant market, rather than one made to equip a great interior. The gilt metal mounts are just rococo, but much stiffer than those in the previous example.

WRITING FURNITURE ✱

This was the time of the bureau-plat. Reading, writing and study were fashionable. It was the time of the 'Encyclopaedists' who published descriptions of everything that they found.

Books and letters were not to be hidden away inside desks; they were to be seen being used – hence the large flat desks known as bureau-plat – *see Fig 2.2d*. The type is quite standard: three drawers in either side and raised on graceful tapering cabriole legs. The example shown is in kingwood (*Dalbergia cearenis*) and is stamped Plée, created Master in 1767. The tops were almost always of leather.

The kidney-shaped table, with a tambour below enclosing three small drawers, is a type of table unique to France – *see Fig 2.2e*. The carcass is veneered in kingwood and the groundwork of the drawers is lacewood. The table is stamped J. L. Cosson, created Master in 1765.

Above top: Fig 2.2c **Black japanned commode, inspired by newly forged trading links with the East.**

Above: Fig 2.2d **A kingwood bureau-plat stamped by the maker, Plée.**

ITALY

The influences that were forming the move away from rococo began in 1750 when the man responsible for the Royal Buildings made a trip to Italy. Shortly after this, books showing Classical remains were published, and some cabinetmakers began to use neo-classic ornament.

This transition from rococo to neo-classic took some 30 years and in some places never happened at all! In the provinces rococo furniture was made up until the end of the century.

Finally, another form of writing table is shown – *see Fig 2.2h*. This bureau à cylindre dates from about 1780 and is also in the Transitional style. After the freedom of the rococo there came about a certain reserve in design circles.

Remember this was only nine years before the French Revolution erupted. The intellectual and idealistic freedom of the 1750s to 1770s was about to spawn anarchy and re-birth. Designs were restrained and different.

Sometimes these tables have slides which provide an occasional surface on which to write letters. They were very much a lady's table, being positioned by the owner's favourite chair. Another very pretty table is shown in *Fig 2.2f*. In this example the top drawer is fitted with a leather-topped writing surface and has compartments for pens and ink.

PATRONAGE

There were many famous Ébénistes in the 18th century – too many to mention. I have, therefore, concentrated on the shapes and types of furniture rather than the makers. However, as luck would have it, the next object is attributed to one of the great masters, Oeben.

J. F. Oeben was made Ébéniste du Roi in 1754 and created Master in 1761. Why, you may wonder, was he made cabinetmaker to the king before he was made Master?

This sort of anomaly was the norm in fashionable society. The patronage of the King was more important than approval of one's work by one's peers. Fashionable makers could in those days do pretty much what they liked and often broke their own guild rules.

The desk shown in *Fig 2.2g* is called a secrétaire à abattant. This means a desk with a 'pull-down' front. It is veneered in kingwood, tulipwood and purpleheart, with green stained sycamore Greek-key design. You will notice that it has the decoration of a Transitional piece and was, in fact, made around 1760.

> *" Books and letters were not to be hidden away inside desks; they were to be seen being used – hence the large flat desks known as bureau-plat "*

Gone are the flowing curves imitating nature: this designer could not be accused of supporting the old regime. He based his decoration on straight lines and good historical precedent – classical egg and dart – but classical perceived as a kind of Golden Age in which democratic city states flourished.

Right: Fig 2.2g **Transitional-style secrétaire à abattant, by J.F. Oeben, circa 1760. This is a desk with a fall front that can be used as a writing surface. Spectacularly veneered in kingwood, tulipwood and purpleheart with sycamore Greek-key motif.**

Below: Fig 2.2h **Transitional-style bureau à cylindre, circa 1780, shows characteristic restraint – a design throwback to more settled classical times.**

RELEVANT DATES

1715	Baroque style ends
1715	Louis XIV dies
1715	Régence style starts
1723	Louis XV comes of age
1723	Régence ends
1725	Catherine the Great ascends throne of Russia
	Rococo style starts
1745	Jacobite rebellion in England and Scotland
1757	Transitional style starts
1760	George III ascends throne of England and Scotland
1762	Rousseau publishes **The Social Contract**
1771	Transitional style becomes less dominant
1773	Boston Tea Party foreshadows American War of Independence
1774	Louis XV dies
1774	Louis XVI ascends
1785	Directoire style starts; the style came into existence before the government that it was named after
1789	French Revolution begins
1793	Louis XVI and Marie Antoinette executed
1793–94	Reign of Terror in France
1795	Directoire rules France
1799	Consulate rules France
1799	Empire style starts

18TH-CENTURY FRENCH FURNITURE PART II

The last part looked at the design influences in the early part of the century. Here we consider pieces made in later years.

My first illustration shows a bureau à cylindre made in the late 1770s by David Roentgen – *Fig 2.3a*. Roentgen, a German, and one of the top-flight makers of the century, moved to Paris, then world centre for the creative arts, in 1780. Technically, therefore, this piece was made prior to his French residency. However, he is such an important maker that its inclusion in this article is warranted.

The style is still just rococo but with certain reservations, particularly the straight-section brass mouldings which could easily be fitted to a Transitional piece. The timbers are mahogany (*Swietenia* spp.), purpleheart (*Peltogyne pubescens*), cherry (*Prunus* spp.), sycamore (*Acer* spp.) and stained boxwood (*Buxus* spp.). The cylinder opens to reveal a pull-out writing slide above the lower 'drawers' which open outwards, hinging back to reveal extra drawers and compartments.

Fig 2.3a **Bureau à cylindre made by German émigré David Roentgen. Opened cylinder reveals writing slide. False drawer-fronts mask drawers and compartments.**

COMPLICATED

Roentgen became Ébéniste du Roi et de la Reine in 1785. The example illustrated – *Fig 2.3a* – with its complicated mechanism, concealed compartments and floral swags in marquetry, is typical of the superb pieces made in the second half of the 18th century for royal and noble clients by the most famous cabinetmakers in the world.

The next illustration – *Fig 2.3b* – shows a Louis XVI bureau à cylindre which is much more neo-classical. Again, the gilt metal mounts are simple in section but gone are the floral swags and the surfaces decorated with marquetry. The timber is mahogany and the only concession to decoration is the use of a plum-pudding mahogany on the cylinder. The swept cabriole leg – which was essentially a serpentine shape, probably inspired by the hind legs of quadrupeds used in art such as lions or deer – has been replaced with a simple geometric turned and fluted leg. This was a maker who believed in restraint, not in the wild ebullience of growing plant forms.

Having just said that the cabriole leg had vanished, I am going to demonstrate the complexities of 18th-century furniture history by showing – in *Fig 2.3d* – an elegant commode which might at first glance seem rococo but which is in fact Louis XV.

SERPENTINE

Although this has serpentine legs, curly mounts and serpentine outline to the quartered kingwood veneer, the fact that all these features are restrained indicates this was made after rococo had ceased to be fashionable.

The next example – *Fig 2.3c* – clearly demonstrates the above features. Still serpentine or cabriole legs, but very little use of other decoration, mainly relying on the timbers to make the piece stand out. This is Transitional, circa 1765, and veneered in kingwood and amaranth.

An item made by another famous Ébéniste – *Fig 2.3e* – is a mahogany console-desserte stamped 'B. Molitor'.

Fig 2.3b **Neo-classical bureau à cylindre, circa 1775, with 'plum pudding' cylinder fall.**

A console-desserte is a side table made to stand against a wall, with the table having a shelf below.

Molitor was one of the last ébénistes of the 18th century. He was created Master in 1787 but had to close his workshop at the time of the French Revolution – he even had to appear before the Revolutionary Tribunal – but he was able to start up again at the end of the Terror. There's nothing rococo about this piece and indeed very little that is neo-classical. The decoration is elegant and reserved Louis XVI. The clock, by the way, dates from the same period and has two revolving rings in enamel, one showing the hours and one showing the minutes.

Top: Fig 2.3c **A kingwood and amaranth small writing-table, Louis XV/XVI Transitional, circa 1765.**

Above: Fig 2.3d **Restrained styling on this commode – veneered in quartered kingwood – suggests post-rococo work.**

Fig 2.3e **This elegant, reserved console-desserte – side-table meant to stand against a wall – is from the hand of B. Molitor, one of the last great ébénistes of the 18th century.**

Left: Fig 2.3f **Louis XVI mahogany jardinière – lead-lined plantholder – a style that has endured into our own times.**

Below left: Fig 2.3g **Louis XVI mahogany writing-table with leather-lined top, circa 1785.**

Below right: Fig 2.3h **Two-tier mahogany table, showing the quiet elegance of the Directoire style.**

We now move to smaller items but they still show the same basic design features of the period. *Fig 2.3g* depicts a Louis XVI mahogany writing table with leather top, circa 1785.

LEAD LINER

Fig 2.3f shows a Louis XVI mahogany jardinière. This useful plant holder – with lead liner – is of a form that continued to be made right up until the present century. The tapering fluted legs and restrained brass beading will be familiar to any cabinetmaker.

My last three illustrations are of pieces made after the Revolution and in the Directoire style. The Directoire was the name of the temporary French Government that existed after the King and prior to the Consulate – which itself predates the Empire period.

Napoleon was the first Consul and the First Emperor. All connections with rococo and Louis XV have vanished. *Fig 2.3h* is of a two-tier mahogany table. There is little to say about this; the whole point of the Directoire style is that it was simple but still French – and, therefore, elegant.

Fig 2.3i is of a telescopic table in tulipwood. This sort of table was used to hold a candelabrum and could be raised or lowered to bring the light to the right position. In the daytime it might be used for displaying flowers or perhaps a

" *The whole point of the Directoire style is that it was simple but still French – and, therefore, elegant* "

piece of porcelain or small item of sculpture.

We end the century with a commode that is pure Directoire – *Fig 2.3j* – almost all geometric ornament and no curves. There is nothing about this that would connect its owner – or maker – to anything related to French royalty or aristocratic privilege. Those things were part of the *ancien régime* (France before 1789), and being a member of that group could mean a visit to Madame la Guillotine! The clock dates from 1800 and is made in a new style, that of Empire.

Left: Fig 2.3i **Tulipwood telescopic stand: by night an adjustable lampstand, by day a pedestal for flowers or sculpture.**

Above right: Fig 2.3j **Curve-free concept and geometric ornaments mark out this commode as pure Directoire.**

18TH-CENTURY FRENCH CHAIRS

This part will address French chairs and the next will deal with chairs made in other European countries. Both take the form of captioned pictures rather than text with pictures. This is because the general shape and construction of chairs remained fairly consistent in both the 18th and 19th centuries. Historical dating is primarily based upon decorative features. These are best illustrated by pictures, hence my selection of as many pictures as possible.

Left: This chair is of the Régence period, circa 1720. The frame is of mortise-and-tenoned beech and has been carved and gilded. There are traces of the curvaceous Baroque – see pages 40–43.

Right: This shows a pair of chairs from the same period, again in beech, but with the decoration, although well proportioned, showing signs of the overcrowding of design elements often associated with rococo – see pages 58–61. The covers are needlework.

This pair of walnut chairs was made about 1725. Asymmetrical elements in the design identify them as rococo. These chairs are covered in tapestry – tapestry is woven, needlework is stitched.

These are a pair of bergères from the middle of the century – most comfortable.

This is very rococo, bold and inelegant. The style is early Louis XV. The covers are of tapestry.

These walnut chairs are classic Louis XV, mid 18th century. The shape is known as 'fauteuil'. These are very elegant chairs.

Here is another comfortable seating arrangement. The frames are in walnut and date from the middle of the century. This was probably made in the provinces. Although the legs are cabriole and the basic shape is Louis XV, there is little decoration and the stretchers are decidedly Baroque. This design is an illustration of the fact that rural cabinetmakers were often 40 years out of date! They made what sold – what their customers wanted, not what was fashionable in Paris.

This is a beautiful rococo fauteuil, circa 1750 – again, a classic chair.

The short grain in the legs of these Transitional chairs makes the design sadly impractical.

A beech chair. We know it was made about 1760 because the maker only received Master in 1758.

A pair of canapés circa 1780. Louis XVI style was typically fluting, leaf-carved blocks, guilloche and ribbon-work. By this time a painted finish had become popular.

This is a beech bergère made in the middle of the century. This more restrained rococo is associated with Louis XV. The chair would normally have a thick, loose seat cushion, and the comfort provided by this and the curled back/arm panels led to the association with rural ease – a bergère is a shepherdess.

A Louis XVI banquette. This is a stool made for placing under a window, and is not for regular use as it is too uncomfortable. Literally translated it means 'little bench'.

A small Louis XV sofa in beech, sometimes called a canapé.

This is a pair of large walnut bergères, simple but classic. Mid 18th century.

Another Louis XVI design.

Fig 2.4q **Painted armchairs, circa 1780, Louis XVI. A design that was much-copied at the end of the 19th century.**

A very elegant set of Louis XVI open armchairs or fauteuils, circa 1780.

These chairs are from a set of tapestry-covered Louis XVI seat furniture, circa 1780.

Fig 2.4r **This is a provincial version of Louis XVI, circa 1780. The timbers are of the correct section, but the lack of decoration probably reflects a lack of funds on the part of the buyer. It even doubles as a small two-seater or a large single-seater.**

Another set of often-copied Louis XVI open armchairs, circa 1780.

This settee is part of the suite of Louis XVI chairs shown opposite, second from top.

A carved and painted fauteuil, circa 1785. The carving on the oval back and on the upsweeps to the arms is now becoming rather serious and symmetrical. This is very late Louis XVI and inclining towards Empire.

18TH-CENTURY NON-FRENCH CHAIRS

This section addresses chairs made in European countries other than France, and again takes the form of captioned pictures rather than text with pictures. Historical dating is primarily based upon decorative features.

Left: This is a Franco-German, mid 18th-century chair in beechwood. The style is basically French but the chair was probably made near the Rhine border as there's a certain heaviness about the decoration and timbers that usually indicates Germanic influences. Note, particularly, the back supports where they join the seat rail.

Right: This is a German chair made around 1740. The bold carving on the frame and the outward-scrolling arms are typical German elements. Although the chairs on this page are non-French, it has to be remembered that almost all designs of the 18th century are based on or influenced by French designs.

Below: Two Italian stools in gilt wood. Included because they are unusual, they date from about 1750 and are full of carved detail. Note the acanthus leaves, which are part of the Corinthian Order – see page 39 – although there was a neo-classical revival at the end of the 18th century, many elements of classical design continued to be used right through from the Baroque period in the 17th century to the neo-classical period in the 18th century.

Left: This is not specifically a chair, but as it is the earliest Continental metamorphic chair and table I have seen, I believe it warrants publication. It is walnut and south German, dating from the second quarter of the 18th century. The folding chair sits inside one end of the carcass behind a false drawer front. The desk itself opens to make a set of library steps.

Below: This is a set of Italian walnut armchairs dating from the early to mid eighteenth century. The basic influence is rococo but the exaggerated curves – the arm supports, for example, look as if they are being squashed downward – give the chairs a more 'plastic' and flowing essence than French chairs of a similar age and design. Note the drop-in seats contained within a moulding. This is a 17th-century feature retained by this maker.

This is a fine set of Italian gilt wood armchairs. They are mid 18th century and have the very Italian characteristic of small-radius scrolled arm-supports, as in the examples above right. The leaf-trail carving on the crest rail is unusual. The fabric is late 20th century.

These entirely German chairs date from the middle of the 18th century. They are gilded on beech frames, and rather ponderous. The outward-scrolling arm is a feature often seen on north-German seat furniture at this time.

Above and left: A set of four Italian sofas made for the Palazzo Carrega-Cataldi in 1742. They are exuberant rococo, with sea-dragon supports and voluptuous mermaids crawling along the crest rail. One of the characteristics of the rococo style is that it is not bound by rigid symmetry. These sofas, though, are both rococo and symmetrical. At first glance they might appear to be Régence, but then one notices the ribbon-tied reeding and the acanthus leaves. These pieces are, in fact, looking forward to the neo-classical style of the late 18th century. I'm afraid they are a prime example of the confusion that can come about by using generalizations to ascribe a decorative motif to a particular period in history.

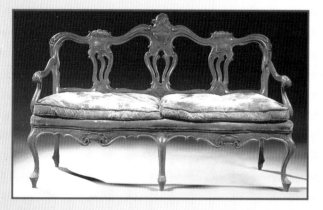

Here is an Italian carved sofa in walnut, made a little later than the armchairs shown on the previous page but still with the distinctive exaggerated scroll work.

This is a carved and painted Italian sofa, circa 1750. It is a simple piece, showing that not all furniture of the 18th century was overgrown with gilt scrolls.

These gilt and Japanned chairs, circa 1750, are restrained rococo. The panels of decoration on the light green ground depict Chinese figures, landscapes and flowers. There are no areas that have too much decoration or too little decoration – all is in proportion. The fabric is modern.

These Italian walnut chairs dating from about 1780 combine both rococo and neo-classical features. Below the seat are neo-classical fluting and entablature; above the seat are rococo scrolls and curves.

These are Italian, mid 18th century. The gilding on the arms of the front chair is worn through to the bole, which gives it a pleasant mellow colour. It almost looks as though the scroll is polished timber, which blends into the adjacent gilded surfaces, but it isn't timber, it is the colour of the clay on which the gold leaf has been laid.

These are Venetian, circa 1750. Notice that the upholstered pad of the back is inserted from behind the chair. This must have made the chair most uncomfortable to sit back in, as the lower rail of the back would stick into the lumbar region. These are pure rococo chairs from Venice, which was the centre of fantastical whimsy in the 18th century.

These are Italian gilt and painted chairs, circa 1780. They are not immediately recognizable as post-rococo because their width and heaviness make them look baroque, but the plain band of cream paint around the seat rail gives the game away: rococo makers would never have left that much space undecorated. The rectangular forms of the back are derived from the classical Orders. Note the woodworm damage – sadly, Italian furniture is prone to woodworm.

We close with a neo-classical chair. These are copies of a design that was made in 1784 for the Villa Borghese in Rome. There is virtually no resemblance to the earlier flowing baroque or rococo. These chairs resemble the klismos chairs from antiquity. At the end of the 18th century a wave of new designs spread through Europe, the 'Golden Age' for European furniture had passed.

ENGLAND 1689 – 1720

Above: Fig 2.6a **Chest-on-stand.**

Below: Fig 2.6b **Chest of drawers.**

ENGLAND SETS THE STANDARD

If the 18th century was significant with regard to Continental furniture then it was world-shattering as far as English furniture was concerned. It's no exaggeration to say that 18th-century English furniture set a standard that has been aspired to throughout the world, both then and now.

NEW CENTURY

The century began with Queen Anne, who ascended in 1702 and ruled to 1714. However, it would be unfair of me not to mention the chests-on-stands which were really William and Mary (1689–1702) pieces that acted as transitional items between the two centuries. The first photograph, *Fig 2.6a*, is of a walnut marquetry cabinet, circa 1690. The style originates from Holland but, as we shall see later, the very English sense of proportion is already evident. This cabinet-on-stand is not over-cluttered with decoration and does not

have excessively turned spirals or exaggerated stretchers and feet. Each design element is in proportion to its neighbour, and thus the whole piece is in proportion to itself.

The idea of putting a containing box on a stand was really a 17th-century concept. *Fig 2.6c*, the coffer-on-stand, circa 1710, is included because, again, this piece shows the sense of proportion in furniture design. It's a japanned coffer – see explanation of 'japanning' on page 36. The idea of a coffer as a piece of furniture is very ancient, this is almost the latest date at which we will see such pieces being made. Collectors' cabinets-on-stands were made in the 19th century, but they are not really of the same origin. This piece was made to show off the 'exotic' japanning. Any object which looked Japanese in the early 18th century was highly sought after as a status symbol. The stand displays the classic scrolled frieze, elegant elongated legs and pad feet. It's 3ft (915mm) high, 1ft 10in (560mm) wide and 12in (305mm) deep. The dimensions are more easily grasped in imperial measurements, because that is what English makers used: these people used a 1in chisel, not a 25mm one.

The next photograph, *Fig 2.6d*, is of a 'seaweed' marquetry chest of drawers on bun feet, 35in (890mm) wide. This is made in walnut and dates from about 1695. The name 'seaweed' is given to the style of marquetry because the thin tendrils of marquetry resemble those of seaweed. Seaweed marquetry clock cases are also found. The peardrop pulls for the drawers are typical of the period. *Fig 2.6e* shows the top in detail. By the way, when looking at any walnut furniture,

Above: Fig 2.6c **Coffer on stand.**

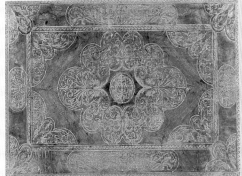

Top: Fig 2.6d **Another chest of drawers.**

Middle: Fig 2.6e **Top view of chest of drawers.**

Above: Fig 2.6f **Bachelor's chest.**

beware of painted figure or grain. The dark swirling lines in the grain are often painted in by polishers, but that is not the case on this piece. *Fig 2.6b* shows a much more ordinary chest of drawers. This is plainer in decoration but still dates from the last years of the 17th century. One might be tempted to think the bracket feet makes it 18th century, but these are later replacements.

UNIQUE

Now we'll look at a type of chest of drawers unique to the early part of the 18th century, the bachelor's chest. The walnut example – *Fig 2.6f* – is formed as a square elevation, 26in wide by 26in high, and 10in deep (660 x 660 x 255mm). These are very elegant proportions: a similar example of the use of proportion are the double-cube rooms

By the beginning of the 18th century, books were becoming more commonplace

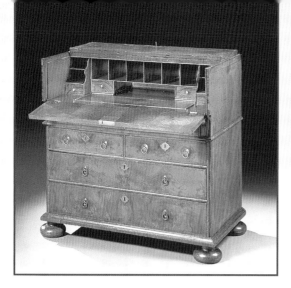

Left: Fig 2.6g **Secretaire bachelor's chest.**

Right: Fig 2.6h **Kneehole desk.**

that were found in architecture. This chest is well-suited for a modern batchelor as it only intrudes into the bedroom by 10in (255mm). The rules of proportion were just being discovered by designers. At first they used the same height as width, but because furniture could not go too high, they found that the available width was limited. As the science of proportion began to develop, the use of the 'golden mean' and other formulae began to be used, allowing designers to make wider objects that were still comfortable to sit or stand at, and also looked good. However, the Queen Anne period is regarded as the 'age of narrow furniture'.

The principle of a bachelor's chest is that the young man needs a combined chest and table for his tiny bed/sitting room. The hinged-top folds over to rest on lopers and can be used for eating, writing or brushing clothes. This example dates from about 1715 and the tall bracket feet are original. Note the brass swan-neck handle has appeared.

DESKS

Let's now move on to desks proper. There are two varieties, the flat top and the sloping top. *Fig 2.6g* nicely shows the transition between the two. This is a walnut chest of drawers below, with a hinged fall and a rising lid revealing a secretaire compartment fitted with pigeon holes and drawers above. It dates from about 1695. There is also a slide between the stationery drawers which reveals a well. This was used to store valuable documents, the slide being concealed under a pile of inconsequential documents! Sometimes the front of the well space is concealed behind a false drawer.

A flat-top kneehole desk – *Fig 2.6h* – is made from walnut and dates from 1710. The elevation is a square, 29 by 29in and 19in deep (737 x 737 x 483mm). One feature of this period is the mouldings around the drawer apertures. This piece has double half-round beads, made of cross-grain walnut; many altered pieces have them in long-grain walnut.

" *It's no exaggeration to say that 18th-century English furniture set a standard that has been aspired to throughout the world, both then and now* "

Left: Fig 2.6i **Narrow bureau bookcase.**

Right: Fig 2.6j **Red lacquer bureau bookcase.**

Far right: Fig 2.6k **Double dome top bureau bookcase.**

BOOKS

By the beginning of the 18th century, books were becoming more commonplace. Just as plates could be stored on the upper shelves of a dresser, books could be stored on a superstructure to a desk. The bureau bookcase had been born! *Fig 2.6i* shows a very elegant narrow walnut example, circa 1715. It's 32in (813mm) wide and has a mirrored door.

Of course, some people didn't want narrow and elegant, they wanted big and showy. *Fig 2.6j* is of such a piece. This is the classic red-lacquer bureau bookcase of the Queen Anne period, 7ft (2134mm) high and half as wide. The tall, narrow divisions are for folio-size books and ledgers. The faux marble columns pull out to reveal secret compartments.

The next illustration, *Fig 2.6k*, is of an unlacquered double dome top version. Again, it's in walnut but with the interior drawers veneered in field maple and ebony. Field maple was used as an alternative to mulberry.

TABLES

There is just enough space to show a few tables. *Fig 2.6l* shows a 2ft 6in (762mm) wide side table with fold-over top in walnut, circa 1695. It has a shaped frieze echoed by the solid stretcher. The central drawer is real but the side drawers are false. The tapering columns are faceted and end in stylized square club feet.

The next table – *Fig 2.6m* – shows a very simple walnut design, probably made five to ten years later. It is 3ft (915mm) wide. The decorative frieze, the undertier and the curious feet have gone but the facetted columns remain. As we approach modern times we will find that there are more and more items to study. With a larger group of items to examine it's possible to sub-divide design features into decades or parts of decades. At first glance it would appear that dating has become easier, but in fact we have come to realize that many pieces of furniture were made with retrospective features included in their design. In this case, although the faceted columns date from the previous two decades, the simple lines of the other features indicate this table was made in the pre-Georgian 'transitional' period, not in the late 17th century.

Fig 2.6n shows a curious throwback to the late baroque period. This is 2ft 10in (864mm) wide. The table was made around 1705, as part of a suite of furniture which is in the Victoria and Albert Museum, London. It has now been painted black but was originally gilded. This table displays a complete contrast to the flowing lines of conventional Queen Anne furniture and also to the classical Palladian style that was waiting in the wings. It's easy to understand that the next generation of owners of grand houses felt all the Restoration and Baroque furniture they had inherited was wildly out of fashion. There was an enormous change in England when George I came to the throne in 1714.

The previous section closed with some early tables, and the general form of those is not often seen nowadays. However, the table shown in *Fig 2.7a* is a well-known design; this is a walnut veneered card table. This design is much copied. The top folds over and the rear legs move backwards on concertina-action, hinged rails to provide a support. The inside of the top is baize lined and the lobed corners are recessed to hold candlesticks. A nice refinement one sometimes finds is the 'guinea well'. These are little hollows in the surface of the opened up top, into which coins can be put in order to keep the winnings tidy. The decorations at the top of the legs are called lappets. The term means 'lapped over'.

Above: Fig 2.7a **Walnut concertina-action card table, 1720.**

MORE TABLES

The next table – *Fig 2.7c* – dates from about 1735 and is made from solid mahogany and has swing legs. The shell decoration harks back to the Queen Anne period, but the form of the table is Georgian. There are two basic configurations for these dining tables, which were made for the next 270 years. One is with four legs, two of which swing; the other is with six legs, usually only two of which are swing legs. The six-legged version is more stable and to be preferred. *Fig 2.7d* shows a larger table with six legs. Although one might think the six legs are the result of having a large top to support, they also produce more stable seating when there are more than three people dining and each one leans on the top, at the port and brandy stage.

One of the wonderful designs of the Georgian period was the tripod table. They come in many varieties some with pivoting tops, some with birdcage tops. The 'birdcage' refers to the cluster of small columns which link a pair of wooden plates which fit onto the top of the main column. The birdcage is a feature that is often faked. The first table – *Fig 2.7b* – is a brass inlaid mahogany table, circa 1745. The lobed and inlaid top is most unusual, the acanthus

carving and the claw and ball feet are more commonly found. The second example is shown in *Fig 2.7e*. It's of mahogany and was made about ten years later. The brass inlay had by that time become unfashionable but carved decoration was still in vogue. This example has a nicely carved rim – some others were 'pie crust', that is with the shape of the edge of a baked pie – and more distinct claws. An offshoot of the tripod table is the 'dumb waiter'. This is basically a three-tier tripod table as shown in *Fig 2.7k*. This example is in mahogany and dates from about 1755.

MORE TABLES

Another type of Georgian table is the side or serving table. This is the forerunner of the sideboard – a marble-topped example is shown in *Fig 2.7f*. This has the shell decoration to the frieze, normally associated with the Queen Anne or George I period, but in this case is George II, circa 1745. When dating a piece one must work on the basis of the most recent design feature, not just the most well-known. Hence the scrolls and the acanthus leaves put the piece into the 1740s.

Fig 2.7b **Tripod table, 1745.**

Top: Fig 2.7c **Mahogany dining table, 1735.**
Middle: Fig 2.7d **Dining table, George II.**
Above: Fig 2.7e **Tripod table, 1755.**

" *One of the wonderful designs of the*
Georgian period was the tripod table.
They come in many varieties some with
pivoting tops, some with birdcage tops "

The final table I'm going to show is *Fig 2.7g*. It is known as
an architect's table. The front legs are divided diagonally
down their length and they, together with the drawer, pull
forward. This reveals a series of compartments for pens,
paints and geometry instruments. The top lifts up
to form a slope onto which a sheet of drawing paper can be
placed. The ability to draw and design things was much
prized in the 18th century. Every 'well-to-do' house would
have an architect's table in the study or library at which
classical design books could be studied and copied.

BEDROOM

Now we move to the bedroom. *Fig 2.7h* shows a tray-top
bedside table in mahogany, circa 1755. Again, these are much
copied. The lower section pulls forward in the same manner
as the architect's table, but this time a commode is revealed.

SOVEREIGNS

1714 – 1727	George I
1727 – 1760	George II

Below the tray-top is a pair of doors. Note the nicely proportioned scrolled edges to the tray top. *Fig 2.7j* shows a mahogany straight-front chest of drawers with brass handles, circa 1750. This example has a brushing slide, and is only 2ft 6in (762mm) wide. It's raised on bracket feet. This is the classic English bedroom chest of drawers.

Fig 2.7i shows another straight-front chest but this one dates from 1730. This is walnut and does not have an overhanging top. The feet and the handles are similar to the previous example. The overhanging top is a most important feature in dating furniture. In very rough terms walnut had ceased to be used by about 1740 and had been replaced by mahogany. Much has been written about the dates of the use of various timbers. It's a complex subject and one which is still being researched.

Next – *Fig 2.7p* – is one example of a Georgian mahogany bureau, circa 1750. This is essentially a chest of drawers with a sloping top. Once again the design has stayed the same for 250 years. I have passed over the subject of bureaux rather briefly because they are well-known and space is limited. More interesting is the bureau bookcase – *Fig 2.7n*. This was made about 1750 and has classic Georgian proportions. Mirror glass was becoming less expensive, as was ordinary glass. Bookcase tops were glazed in either material; solid doors were much less common. The moulding around the frieze at the top is called 'dentil' moulding – from the Latin for 'tooth'. The handles at the sides are not really intended for lifting, they are decorative. Note, never trust a 'lifting'

Left 1: Fig 2.7f **Side table, 1745.**
Left 2: Fig 2.7g **Architect's table, 1750.**
Left 3: Fig 2.7h **Bedside table, 1755.**
Left 4: Fig 2.7i **Straight-front chest, 1730.**
Below: Fig 2.7j **Straight-front chest, 1750.**
Right: Fig 2.7k **Dumb waiter, 1755.**

handle on an antique without checking it first; it can be embarrassing and painful when the screws pull out and the item crashes onto your toes.

TALLBOYS

One piece of distinctively Georgian furniture no longer copied is the 'tallboy' or chest-on-chest. *Fig 2.7o* shows a lovely example with wonderful flame veneers. This piece was made about 1760. The corners are canted and fluted, as is the frieze; dentils are present on the cornice and the swan-neck handles have plain, round pommels instead of backplates as found in the earlier pieces. *Fig 2.7l* shows a similar piece of furniture made about ten years earlier. This is a linen press. The word 'press' means 'cupboard'. The top doors open to reveal sliding trays onto which clothes were placed. The features that indicate it's slightly earlier than the previous piece are the 'architectural' cornice – early Georgian was the time of the 'Great Architects' like William Kent – the heavier handles and the scrolled ogee bracket feet. Once again, the figure on the mahogany is impressive.

AND FINALLY

My final piece – *Fig 2.7m* – is almost a piece of architecture. Although it contained books when photographed, it is in fact a break-front display cabinet, circa 1750. The term 'break-front' refers to the centre section which is further forward than the two sides. That is a feature derived from classical architecture, as is the 'broken' pediment, the egg and dart carved mouldings and the concave spandrels joining the top of the sides to the main piece.

Below: Fig 2.7l **Linen press, 1750.**
Below right: Fig 2.7m **Broken pediment bookcase, 1750.**
Far right: Fig 2.7n **Mirrored bureau bookcase, 1750.**

> " *One piece of distinctively Georgian furniture that is no longer copied is the 'tallboy' or chest-on-chest* "

Top: Fig 2.7o **Tallboy, 1760.**
Above: Fig 2.7p **Bureau, 1750.**

ENGLAND 1760 – 1770

The middle Georgian period was a time of consolidation. The design experiments had come in the early Georgian years, returning again in the late Georgian years, but the middle years were a time of stability, solidarity and righteous well-fed country squires. All pieces shown are made from mahogany unless stated otherwise.

Left: Fig 2.8a **Partners' desk, circa 1760.**

Below: Fig 2.8b **Combined chest of drawers and dressing table, circa 1760.**

WELL-FED

The well-fed needed solid furniture: this will become very obvious when we examine seat furniture! *Fig 2.8a* shows a robust desk commonly called a 'partners' desk'. It's 5ft (1524mm) wide and 38in (965mm) deep and dates from about 1760. The theory is that business partners should have nothing to hide from each other and therefore they would be happy to share the same writing desk. Then each could see what the other was up to! This example is an undecorated, solid piece of furniture; just what entrepreneurs from the flowering of the Industrial Revolution would have wanted.

The standard straight-front chest of drawers remained fairly unchanged. An example from about 1760 is shown in *Fig 2.8b*. It's a combined chest of drawers and dressing table, the top drawer which is fitted for bottles and other containers has a drop down front which can be supported on the lopers which are either side of the second drawer. It's raised on standard Georgian bracket feet.

Fig 2.8d shows a mahogany bowl stand, circa 1760. This is a stand for a washbowl and would have stood in a bedroom. The general form is that of rococo curves with leaf ornamentation, but it is a light and airy shape which heralds a change. Within 10 years, heavy furniture would be unfashionable, and light, airy, whimsical pieces would be the order of the day. This particular piece almost looks as if it could be blown away in a strong wind!

*" The middle Georgian period
was a time of consolidation "*

Left: Fig 2.8c **Tea paraphernalia: an urn stand, 1770.**

Above: Fig 2.8d **Mahogany bowl stand, circa 1760.**

Below: Fig 2.8e **A plain and simple mahogany dining-table, circa 1760.**

TABLES AND TEA

Fig 2.8e shows a plain and simple mahogany dining table made about 1760. The table is formed from three separate pieces of furniture. There are two D-shaped ends which are supported on turned columns of the type found on tripod tables. These D-shaped ends can be stood against the wall to make a pair of console or pier tables, or they can be joined together to make a small oval table seating four persons. The central section is made as a drop-flap table. When not in use as a dining table this drop-flap table would stand against the wall as a side table. The entire dining table is 2ft 4in (711mm) wide and 7ft 6in (2286mm) long.

The practice of tea drinking had its own etiquette and furniture. One such piece of tea paraphernalia was the urn stand. An example dating from 1770 is shown in *Fig 2.8c*. The silver-plated urn would stand on the top and a teapot could be placed on the little pull-out slide below.

The item shown in *Fig 2.8g* is a firescreen, and its purpose is to protect the face from the heat of a fire. The needlework screen can slide up or down the pole until at the right height to protect the face but allow the fire's heat to reach the rest of the room. It was made around 1765, note the profiled, opposed C-scroll legs and fluting on the column. If it had been made earlier it would have had a simpler, more robust column.

The next two items are chests of drawers in the London style. Previous pieces have been rather provincial, and as such have lagged a few years behind London designs. *Fig 2.8f* shows a serpentine-fronted chest of drawers, from about 1765. This is quite different from the last chests of drawers featured on pages 78–81, all of which were straight-fronted and plain. The bracket feet still survive, but are ornamented with ogee shapes. Side handles are still used, but will not continue for many more years. The main handles are decorated with neo-classical reeding and beading. The canted corners have blind fret which was introduced by Chippendale in the preceding decade; beaded scrolled brackets and scrolled leaf decoration. It is 3ft 6in (1067mm) wide and a very delicate 22in (559mm) deep. *Fig 2.8k* shows a serving table dating from about 1765. The serving table was the precursor of the sideboard. The other ancestor of the sideboard was the pedestal and urn – *Fig 2.8h*. The urns contained divisions to store cutlery, ice for wine coolers or other dining-room-related contents. Sometimes the urns were constructed separately from the pedestals, sometimes the pedestals and the urns were built

Top: Fig 2.8f **Serpentine-fronted chest of drawers, circa 1765.**

Above: Fig 2.8g **Firescreen, circa 1765.**

Right: Fig 2.8h **Pedestals and urn, circa 1770.**

as one item. The example shown has ornamentation dating from the start of the neo-classical period, about 1770. The wide drawers at the base of the pedestals are cellarette drawers. The pedestals are 18in (457mm) square and 3ft (914mm) high.

AND FINALLY

Fig 2.8j shows a pair of candle stands or torchères. These were placed behind a chair in order that the sitter could read easily, or in other convenient places where the light of a candelabrum was needed. Sometimes they were also used to display ornaments such as porcelain vases, figurines or small urns.

Finally, *Fig 2.8i* shows the detail of a fitted dressing-table drawer made in about 1760. The fitted drawer has a leather-covered slide above the adjustable mirror and inlaid compartments. A pen drawer is formed in the side of the main drawer. Such a piece of furniture combines both desk and clothes storage – the Georgians were very skilled at making multi-purpose furniture.

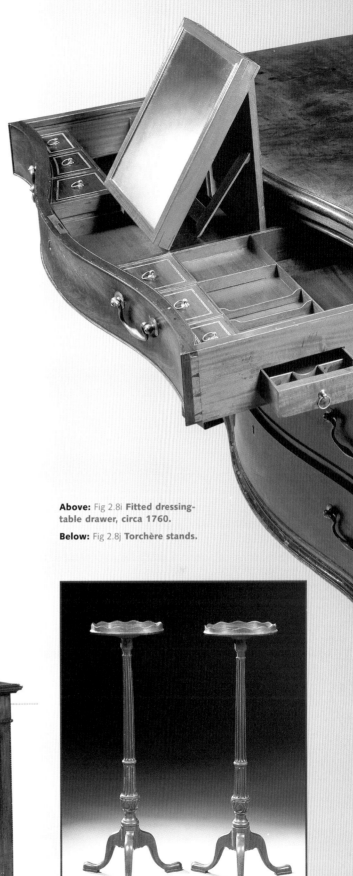

Above: Fig 2.8i **Fitted dressing-table drawer, circa 1760.**

Below: Fig 2.8j **Torchère stands.**

" *Tea became very popular in the early 18th century and a ritual about drinking tea developed such that special china and furniture was produced* "

Fig 2.8k **Serving table, circa 1765.**

Fig 2.9a **Tallboy, late 1760s.**

As we move into the last years of the 18th century, change comes very fast. The mahogany tallboy or chest-on-chest – *see Fig 2.9a* – was made in the late 1760s. The satinwood bow-front clothes press – *Fig 2.9c* – was made in 1790. Both pieces of furniture serve the same purpose but are widely different in shape and decoration. The chest-on-chest has retained basically the same shape for about 100 years. The individual parts of the piece are structurally sound and robust. Then along came the Adam brothers and by 1777 they were able to write in *The Works in Architecture of Robert and James Adam* that they were responsible for 'an almost total change' in design. Shapes became more important than function. Just look at the feet in *Fig 2.9c*: imagine how heavy that press is, to be supported on such delicate legs!

Before we leave the robust years, I would like to show another item of mid-Georgian furniture. *Fig 2.9b* shows a mahogany wine-cooler, made about 1768. It stands 2ft 3in high and 25in wide, and solid-brass banding and side lifting handles place its design derivation firmly in the pre-Adam period.

HOUR OF THE DAY

Fig 2.9e shows a little bonheur-du-jour dating from 1770. The name 'bonheur-du-jour' means 'good hour of the day' perhaps referring to the hour of the day when letters were read and written. This little desk is influenced by French designs, but is in the style of work associated with John Cobb (flourished circa 1750–1778). The use of marquetry had died out after the William and Mary period, but was revived in the neo-classical late 18th century.

Fig 2.9f shows a harewood and marquetry cabinet-on-stand. Again, this piece is influenced by French designs. It dates from about 1780 and is 4ft 3in (1295mm) high and 1ft 8in (508mm) wide. 'Harewood' is the term given to fiddle-back sycamore that has been stained to give a greenish-grey colour. The interior is fitted with pigeon holes and drawers. The marquetry panel depicts a classical female figure reading, which gives a clue as to the use of the cupboard. In some circles reading was not considered to be a suitable

Photo 2.9b **Wine cooler, circa 1768.**

" As we move into the last
years of the 18th century,
change comes very fast "

Top: Fig 2.9c **Linen press, 1790.**
Above: Fig 2.9d **Commode, 1790.**

pastime for ladies; this cupboard would have allowed the
books and letters to be locked away if the lady of the house
suddenly received an old-fashioned visitor!

SHAPELY

Now we move on to the curvaceous 90s. Dating from about
1790, *Fig 2.9d* shows a satinwood and harewood commode.
Some commodes are fitted with sliding trays or drawers and
are used in place of chests of drawers. Indeed, on the
Continent a chest of drawers for the bedroom is called a
'commode'. This piece of furniture has shelves and was
intended for the drawing room. There is a drawer above the
cupboards which can only be opened by using the key as a
handle, as is the case with the doors below. It is 5ft 2in
(1575mm) wide and 2ft (610mm) deep.

Another commode from the same period is shown in
Fig 2.9g on page 88. This is very French in style. England
was at war with France at the end of the century, but they
were at war with the revolutionary government, not with the

Top: Fig 2.9e **Bonheur-du-jour, 1770.**
Above: Fig 2.9f **Cabinet-on-stand, circa 1780.**

Fig 2.9g **Commode, 1790.**

artists, designers and patrons of the arts. The tribulations of those who patronized the furniture-makers served to popularize French design. Back to reality now with a simple, hanging corner-cupboard from 1785 – *Fig 2.9h*. It's 3ft 6in (1067mm) high and 2ft 9in (838mm) wide. Again, the keys are used as handles – handles would have spoiled the line of the ornamentation. The basic timber is mahogany, with satin-birch pilasters, urns, wheat ears and shells.

Another simple but elegant piece of furniture is the side cabinet – *Fig 2.9i*. In the late 18th century, furniture didn't have to be essential, it could exist just because it looked attractive. This mahogany side-cabinet, dating from 1785, served no vital purpose in the drawing room other than to look good and display ornaments on its top surface. Pleated silk has been used to form the panels of the doors. By 1790 mass production of pottery and porcelain was taking place. Other decorative objects, such as lacquered and enamelled ware, were also being made; clocks and bronzes were more available. The well-to-do middle classes needed somewhere to display their decorative objects. The result was side cabinets, pier tables and display cabinets.

Standard pieces of furniture were still being made, as shown by the secrétaire press in *Fig 2.9j*. This piece is attributed to the firm Gillow's, whose name is synonymous with good design and good craftsmanship. The form is that of a solid mahogany secrétaire cabinet, made in about 1788. The selection of the timbers is excellent and the interior layout is well-proportioned. Lip service is paid to the swept foot, but in fact the line of the foot is such that a long-grain stub foot can be fitted behind the face veneer, thus taking the full weight quite happily. This demonstrates the difference between furniture designed with input from cabinet-makers, as was Gillow's, and furniture designed by men who drew designs but never lifted a chisel!

A mahogany breakfront bookcase is shown in *Fig 2.9k*; this is 8ft 9in high, 8ft 1in wide and 1ft 10in deep (2667 x 2464 x 559mm) and dates from 1785. The term 'breakfront' refers to the way in which the central section of drawers and cupboards are brought forward in front of the line of the flanking side sections. Fashion is satisfied by the curving glazing bars and the neo-classical pediment.

NEO-CLASSICAL

A very neo-classical cabinet-on-stand is shown in *Fig 2.9l*. This piece is made in rosewood and kingwood, stands 4ft 9in (1448mm) high and 2ft (610mm) wide and was made around 1790. The reeding on the legs and around the frieze is a fresh and new design feature for the late 18th century, the three urn finials are also very neo-classical, but similar to the urn finials found on bookcases made in the first quarter of the 18th century.

Once again, it's not possible to date an item by firm rules using single features, the most significant thing about this piece is the timber used – rosewood began to be used in large quantities at the end of the 18th century. The cabinet contains small drawers, and could be classed as a 'collector's cabinet'.

The final photograph, *Fig 2.9m* shows a little secrétaire cabinet in West Indian satinwood. There are two distinct species of satinwood. East Indian satinwood (*Chloroxylon swietenia*) is regarded as the 'lesser' of the two woods and often has a wilder grain. East Indian satinwood is very commonly found on Edwardian furniture. West Indian satinwood (*Zanthoxylum flavum*) loses its vibrant colour with age but the resultant paleness is regarded as attractive. Both woods appear to look like folded silk or satin – but some cuts reveal this figure more obviously than others. West Indian satinwood was imported into England as early as the 17th century but appears to have been used for marquetry rather than sheet veneering. It was not until about 1770 that this wood was used in large quantities in British furniture. The oval panels on the cabinet are formed from contemporary coloured prints after Angelica Kauffmann. This piece shows the complete transition from robust mid-Georgian to simple but elegant restrained neo-classicism.

> *The well-to-do middle classes needed somewhere to display their decorative objects. The result was side cabinets, pier tables and display cabinets*

Left: Fig 2.9k **Breakfront bookcase, 1785.**
Top: Fig 2.9l **Collector's cabinet, 1790.**
Bottom: Fig 2.9m **Secrétaire cabinet, 1790.**

ENGLAND 1770 – 1790
PART II

The late 18th century was regarded as 'The Age of Enlightenment' and in 1791 Thomas Paine's book, *Rights of Man*, was published. Towards the end of the century furniture-makers' clients had much more free time, and furniture was made that satisfied popular taste and activities. A variety of tables appeared for occasional or specific use. Also, the major design books were published between 1754 and 1794. The specific purpose of these books was to provide a visual listing of various types of furniture and furniture decoration; the result was a burgeoning of different types of object.

Left: Fig 2.10a **Yew-wood tripod table, circa 1770.**

Top: Fig 2.10b **Side table, circa 1775.**

Above: Fig 2.10c **Mahogany serving table, circa 1780.**

TABLES

The first example in *Fig 2.10a* is a yew-wood tripod table, 1ft 8in (508mm) wide, made in about 1770. It is light and delicate, ornamented with scrolled legs and a spiral-fluted baluster. *Fig 2.10b* shows a side table, 4ft 9in (1448mm) wide, dating from about five years later. This has a marquetry top raised on tapering panelled legs below a frieze decorated with swags and paterae. Both these pieces were motivated by neo-classical design features. *Fig 2.10f* shows a far more recognizably Georgian mahogany two-flap table, 3ft 2in by 2ft 4in (965 by 711mm) when open. It was made in the 1780s and is known as a 'Pembroke' table. The name is derived from the person who first designed and commissioned this style of table. There is some unresolved academic dispute about whether this was the Earl of Pembroke or, as Sheraton states in his *Cabinet Dictionary* of

1803: "The lady who first gave orders for one". The fact remains that whoever 'invented' it, the Pembroke table became very popular in the late-Georgian period and every drawing room had at least one, and sometimes two, tables of this kind.

The mahogany serving table shown in *Fig 2.10c* looks traditional Georgian but comfortably accommodates the neo-classical decoration. It was made around 1780 in Ireland and is 6ft (1829mm) wide by 2ft 9in (838mm) deep. Georgian furniture made in Ireland is much sought after. The decoration is very positive and elegant. A plainer form of serving table with a marble top, also dating from about 1780, is shown in *Fig 2.10d*. This maker had heard that classical decoration included fluting and paterae but hasn't really got the sense of design and proportion that the other exponents of classical decoration have demonstrated.

CURVES

A return to serpentine curves is shown in the next two photos. The mahogany card table – *Fig 2.10g* – was made circa 1785 and is 3ft 3in (991mm) wide. This is a simple card table that is almost Louis XV. The top swivels and opens, one rear leg swings out to support the top, and a secret drawer is revealed behind the swing leg. *Fig 2.10h* shows a small mahogany serving table, 3ft 9in (1143mm) wide made at about the same date. This maker has managed to retain the mid-Georgian robustness but include the popular curved outlines. Although there are handles and a keyhole, there is no drawer – it's a dummy feature.

Top: Fig 2.10f **Pembroke table made in the 1780s.**
Middle: Fig 2.10g **Mahogany card table, circa 1785.**
Bottom: Fig 2.10h **Table, circa 1785.**

Top: Fig 2.10d **Serving table with marble top, dating from about 1780.**

Above: Fig 2.10e **Mahogany oval library writing table made in the 1790s.**

Above: Fig 2.10i **Pembroke table, circa 1790**

Right: Fig 2.10j **Card table, circa 1790.**

Fig 2.10e on page 91 shows a mahogany oval library writing-table, 4ft 6in (1372mm) wide. This is a nicely set out piece of furniture with various luxuries. It has a tooled-leather top, lockable frieze drawers inlaid with ivory labels showing pairs of letters of the alphabet and brass castors so that it can be moved easily. It's similar to a 'rent' table – which has labelled drawers for individual tenants' accounts – and indeed it may have been used as such. Rent tables normally have revolving tops, so the landlord can sit in the same place and merely spin the top until he is faced with the correct drawer.

CONVENTIONAL AND UNCONVENTIONAL

In *Fig 2.10i* we see a more conventional Pembroke table, again made around 1790, in West Indian satinwood. The cross-banding is in kingwood. The use of kingwood is a continental touch. The arises have an ebony line let into them which contributes to the neo-classical look. *Fig 2.10j* shows a card table from the same date in figured West Indian satinwood. The feet are known as spade feet and have unusual, slightly concave sides. *Fig 2.10k* shows a piece made in mahogany and satinwood. It's a rather unusual combined firescreen and writing surface. It's 3ft 5in (1041mm) high and 15in (381mm) wide. The decoration on the inside of the doors are printed transfers that have been applied to the surface and then polished over with shellac. Transfer printing originated on ceramics but this is an example of a trend that was to become very fashionable in the 19th century, using the decorative methods of other media on wooden furniture.

Fig 2.10l shows a novel form of desk in West Indian satinwood. It is 2ft 10in (864mm) wide and has a tambour top revealing a leather surface below which is a writing slide. The tambour is a Continental idea for enclosing a desk but remember that much of the decoration in late 18th-century furniture is more Continental in origin than British. After all, 'classical' designs did originate in Italy and Greece although they were reinterpreted by later architects. It would appear the maker of this desk felt that the novelty of the tambour

was sufficient to sell it, for there is no other decoration – indeed, it presages utilitarian restraint.

Fig 2.10m shows a pretty little pair of console tables, 25in (635mm) wide. Made around 1790 they are decorated with spiral trails of painted flowers on cream legs. The tops are veneered in a fan design with purpleheart segments bordered by boxwood and kingwood bandings. There is some

Fig 2.10k
A rather unusual combined firescreen and writing surface.

Above left: Fig 2.10l **Desk in West Indian satinwood.**

Above: Fig 2.10m **Console tables, circa 1790.**

confusion between console and pier tables; the rule is that if a table has to be screwed to the wall it's a console table. These three-legged tables could not be used to stand porcelain on without securing them to the wall, hence they are console tables.

Fig 2.10n shows a standard four-pillar mahogany dining-table. It is 4ft 9in (1448mm) wide and 15ft 9in (4800mm) long. This example was made around 1790, but is a traditional and popular design that began in the late 18th century and has been made almost continually ever since.

Fig 2.10n **Standard four-pillar mahogany dining table, circa 1790.**

A SELECTION OF DESIGN BOOKS PUBLISHED IN THE 18TH CENTURY

The Gentleman and Cabinetmaker's Director,
T. Chippendale, 1754

The Universal System of Household Furniture: Consisting of above 300 designs in the most elegant taste, both useful and ornamental,
W. Ince and J. Mayhew, 1759–62

The Works in Architecture of Robert and James Adam,
R. and J. Adam, 1777

The Cabinetmaker and Upholsterer's Guide,
A. Hepplewhite and Co., 1788

Designs for Household Furniture,
T. Shearer, 1788

The Cabinetmaker and Upholsterer's Drawing Book,
T. Sheraton, 1791–3

In this section I would like to present a showcase of items made by, or influenced by, some of the great makers of the 18th century. It's not exhaustive: it merely dips into the subject and I have more photographs than there is space for. For this reason I've not written much about the makers (their biographies are available elsewhere). Rather, I will concentrate on the physical features of the objects themselves. Bear in mind the phrase 'made by' does not necessarily imply the person concerned actually made the furniture. Some of those illustrated could, and did, make furniture but for the purposes of the historical study of this period, pieces are attributable to workshops rather than individuals.

Above: These giltwood pedestals, circa 1715, are after a design in Daniel Marot, Nouveaux Livres d 'Orfeuverie, 1713. Marot is not well known as a designer, but was a major figure at the beginning of the century. These shells, scrolls and bellflowers, all late Baroque, are the precursors of work associated with William Kent.

KENT

WILLIAM KENT was born in 1684 and died in 1748. He was probably the first English architect to design the larger structures of a house and its interior as well as the movable furniture inside. Visually his work, even with small pieces of furniture, is very architectural, incorporating columns, cornices and pediments.

Above: An example of the architectural style associated with William Kent, circa 1735.

Below: A West Indian satinwood and painted commode, circa 1790, the panel in the manner of Angelica Kaufmann.

Above: Moving slightly out of the rectilinear architectural style, this console table, circa 1740, is after a design by William Jones, published in The Gentleman or Builder's Companion, 1739, which was among the earliest published collections by any English furniture designer.

KAUFFMANN

ANGELICA KAUFFMANN, 1741 to 1807, was a Swiss artist who specialized in classical compositions. She came to London in 1766 and worked for the Adam Brothers. Her husband, Antonio Zucchi, is less well known, and also worked for Robert and James Adam.

Above: This bookcase, circa 1760, possibly by Thomas Chippendale (1718–79), has glazing bars and decorative mouldings around the doors which are similar to those found on other examples of Chippendale's work.

Below: This bookcase, circa 1760, has been made to a design in The Gentleman and Cabinetmaker's Directory, **which was published in 1754 by Thomas Chippendale.**

Below: A carved pine overdoor, circa 1760 from Harewood House, Yorkshire. Chippendale made much of the furniture for this house as well as some of the carved architectural joinery. I include it as an oddity which demonstrates the – now lost – relationship between furniture makers, architects, designers and joiners.

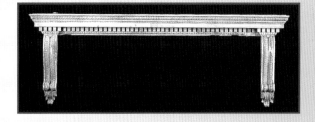

Below: A pier table, circa 1770, attributed to Thomas Chippendale. The quality of the decoration, the range and choice of timbers used, and the overall balance of design all point to Chippendale's work.

Below: A side table in the manner of Thomas Chippendale, circa 1785. This table was made for Farnley Hall, Yorkshire, which was very close to the Chippendales' family home. The decoration is of a quality and style associated with Chippendale's workshop and may have been undertaken under the direction of Thomas Chippendale the Younger, 1749–1822.

Above: A harewood and marquetry pier table, circa 1775, attributed to William Moore, Dublin.

WILLIAM INCE and JOHN MAYHEW flourished between 1758 and 1810. Their address was given in 1779 as Marshall Street, Carnaby Market, in Soho, London. Their work is often decorated with formal, but extensive and beautifully executed marquetry, and noticeably elegant overall shapes.

Above: A pair of console tables, circa 1780, in the manner of Mayhew and Ince.

MOORE

WILLIAM MOORE was active in the years 1782 to 1815. Moore learnt the trade in Mayhew and Ince's workshop and then moved to Dublin. His announcement in the *Dublin Evening Post* runs: *"William Moore most respectfully acknowledges the encouragement he has received, begs leave to inform those who may want Inlaid work, that by his close attention to business and his instructions to his men, he has brought the manufacture to such perfection to be able to sell... Every article in the inlaid Way, executed on shortest notice, and hopes from his long experience at Messrs. Mayhew and Ince, his remarkable fine coloured woods, and elegant finished work, to meet the approbation of all who shall please to honour him with their commands."*

The wording of the advertisement is interesting in that it shows that Georgian makers had many of the same problems to deal with as modern makers do, namely attention to detail, sub-contracted work, short notice and so on. It also refers to *"fine coloured woods"* – this is further evidence that our ancestors wanted bright furniture; the brown, distressed look, so beloved of connoisseurs and collectors is not the look that Georgian buyers expected.

Right: A mahogany chest of drawers, circa 1780, in the manner of Mayhew and Ince.

Left: A rare Irish West Indian satinwood, harewood, ripple sycamore and marquetry cabinet, circa 1785, almost certainly by William Moore of Dublin.

Above: These are a pair of pier tables, circa 1775, in the manner of Mayhew and Ince.

BROOKSHAW

GEORGE BROOKSHAW's address was 48, Great Marlborough Street, Soho, London. He flourished between 1770 and 1790 and numbered the Prince of Wales among his patrons. He is recorded as having worked at the Prince's residence, Carlton House, between 1783 and 1786.

LANGLOIS

PIERRE LANGLOIS is recorded as working in Tottenham Court Road, London, and he *"makes all sorts of fine cabinets and commodes made and inlaid in the politest manner... at the lowest prices"* according to his Trade Card. Another anecdote recorded in a letter to Horace Walpole in 1766 is that the writer, George Montague, saw in Langlois's workshop *"three-quarters of the Japan [lacquer panels] that you gave Langlois to make into commodes are still there!... 'Tis a burning shame."* No change there, then: cabinetmakers put aside jobs that they don't want to do until the client gets really cross – even if the client is the fourth earl of Orford, creator of Strawberry Hill Gothic, a famous author and the son of a Prime Minister.

Right: A painted commode, circa 1775, attributed to George Brookshaw. Brookshaw specialized in botanical painted furniture and it's believed that this piece was commissioned at the same time that Robert Adam was working for the owner's family. Adam would certainly have approved of the neo-classical ornamentation.

Above: This commode, circa 1760, is in the manner of Pierre Langlois, who worked in England. The fine-quality lacquer shows Japanese scenes without the usual overcrowding of motifs so common in European copies of Oriental designs. At first glance this piece would appear to be French but it is, in fact, English.

Right: A lady's writing table, East Indian satinwood and marquetry, made around 1795, after a design by Thomas Sheraton, from The Cabinetmaker and Upholsterer's Drawing Book, 1793. The upper panel protects the face from the heat of the fire, as does a firescreen.

Above: A harewood bonheur-du-jour, circa 1795, by Gillow's of Lancaster, England.

Above: A pier table, circa 1770, in the manner of Robert Adam.

CHAPTER

THREE

The Twilight of Craftmanship

ENGLISH CHAIRS
1700 – 1765

Chairs now began to be made with much more comfort in mind. Instead of having a solid or caned seat with an attached cushion, a webbed and upholstered loose frame was made to be dropped into the main chair frame. This 'drop-in' seat became the standard approach to chair design.

Left: A walnut armchair, circa 1710. The needlework is contained within the cross-grain lippings around the seat and the back.

Above and right: This is a walnut chair-back settee, circa 1720. The double-chair form went out of fashion later in the century. Note the carvings, particularly the eagle-head terminals to the arms. Again, the seat rail is faced with cross-grain lippings.

A pair of mahogany or red walnut side chairs, circa 1720. Note the difficulty found by an earlier restorer in matching the back timbers on the chair in the foreground.

Below: A walnut corner-chair, circa 1725. Corner chairs were made in the first half of the 18th century and again at the end of the 19th century: beware of confusing the two. The veneering and construction of the seat rail, especially at the difficult front-leg joint, will usually determine the age.

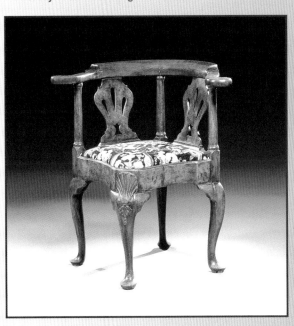

Below: A pair of carved and gilded side-chairs. The front chair is circa 1730; the rear chair is a 19th-century copy. They show a good example of strapwork decoration. The later chair is identified by a maker's stencil on the underside. How convenient it would be if all makers marked their replicas! In fact there are tiny differences within the decoration and in the carving of the gesso. The later chair is less crisply carved, probably indicating that the gilder was working to a price constraint and therefore had a limit to the hours he could spend on the job.

Below: A carved walnut stool, circa 1730. The wave-like carving around the rail is known as 'Vitruvian scrolls'.

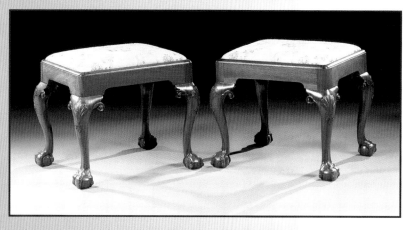

A pair of mahogany stools, circa 1740. This is a very popular pattern that is still found today.

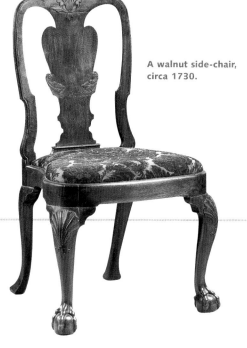

A walnut side-chair, circa 1730.

A pair of walnut side-chairs, circa 1740. Notice that the fronts of the back uprights, the splat – pierced but still a general 'baluster' shape – and the seat rail are all veneered.

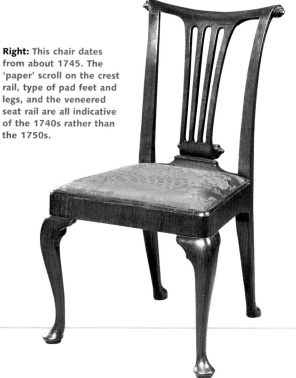

Right: This chair dates from about 1745. The 'paper' scroll on the crest rail, type of pad feet and legs, and the veneered seat rail are all indicative of the 1740s rather than the 1750s.

A mahogany dining chair, circa 1750. Notice how significant changes in the decoration are beginning to appear as we get later in the century. The seat rail is still curved but the stub of the leg is no longer hidden and over-veneered.

Below: A pair of carved mahogany library armchairs, circa 1750. By this date the seats are overstuffed and close-nailed.

Above: These are rather standard, provincial chairs dating from about 1750. The pierced and then entwined backs have been copied from London examples, but the legs are firmly rooted in the preceding decade.

Right: A mahogany library armchair, circa 1765. This has scrolled toes, as do the stools at far right, with acanthus leaf and cabochon decoration. 'Cabochon' refers to the small, oval, uncarved areas in the centre of the arm decoration and the centre of the front seat rail. Cabochon is really a jewellery term for a polished but not faceted gem, which shows how the decorative arts borrow design elements from one another.

Above: This is a pair of wonderful mahogany stools, circa 1760. The scroll feet may look French in style, but these are definitely English stools with English rococo decoration.

ENGLISH CHAIRS
1760 – 1800

Above: A pair of mahogany library armchairs, circa 1760. They have thin-section timbers, producing elegant lines, but avoid the weakness associated with deep curves. The seats of all these mid-Georgian chairs are wider than those of an equivalent chair today, possibly because Georgian posteriors were broader, or maybe to allow for flowing frock coats and wide dresses.

Right: Mahogany dining chairs circa 1760, with pierced interlaced splats. The crest-rail is carved with drapery and tassels.

A mahogany triple-chairback settee, circa 1760. The design of the splat is similar to one published by Thomas Chippendale in 1754. This was a rather cumbersome form of settee which lost favour in the later years of the century.

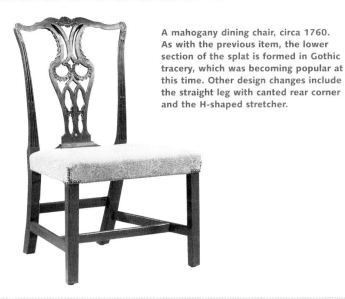

A mahogany dining chair, circa 1760. As with the previous item, the lower section of the splat is formed in Gothic tracery, which was becoming popular at this time. Other design changes include the straight leg with canted rear corner and the H-shaped stretcher.

A pair of carved mahogany library armchairs circa 1765. These are the normal form: robust, strong chairs with simple decoration. Note the nice small castors. Sometimes these are recessed into the bottom of the leg.

Below: A mahogany dining chair, circa 1760. The legs and back uprights are carved with blind Gothic fretwork decoration. The term 'blind' refers to the fact that the decoration is lightly carved over the surface of the timber; the carving has a front and no back. The decoration is formed by what is left after the adjacent material has been carved away. The background material has simply been lowered by ⅛in (3mm) or so. Cheap forms of blind fret are made by gluing pierced fretwork onto a solid ground, then hiding the glue line with dirty wax to make it look as though the piece has been carved from the solid.

Below: A pair of mahogany library armchairs, circa 1760. These are almost identical to a set of 14 chairs known to have been supplied by Thomas Chippendale in 1759 for the Earl of Dumfries. They are so light and airy, especially the buttoning of the fabric so close to the moulding on the seat rail, that they almost look 19th-century. Compare them to other armchairs illustrated and you can see how distinctive and revolutionary Chippendale's designs were.

A pair of mahogany library armchairs, circa 1765. Notice the Gothic blind fret and the pierced spandrel brackets joining the legs to the rails. On better quality chairs the central stretcher is dovetailed into the side stretchers.

Above: One of a set of 14 mahogany chairs, circa 1765. The set contained two armchairs and 12 side chairs. They are rather Continental in style, but the construction and restrained curves confirms their origin as English. Continental chairs often have pegged joints; English chairs, of this and later periods, had glued joints. In general the frame makers used better cabinetwork on English chairs.

Above: A mahogany window seat, circa 1770. The carved decoration on the facings is known as gadrooning or nulling. It consists of carved 'tongues' alternated with flutes: sometimes the flutes are so narrow that they merely consist of the trough or valley between the raised-up 'tongues', all of which is usually sloped to left or right.

Above: Mahogany armchairs, circa 1775. These are now moving away from the earlier Georgian designs and show the influences of the Adam style. The stick splats are carved with flower-heads and leafage resembling palm foliage.

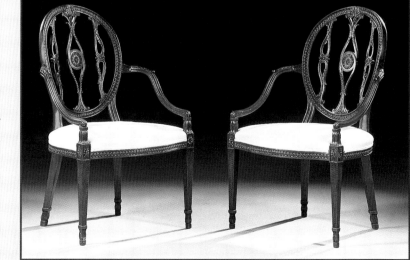

Right: Mahogany armchairs, circa 1775. The neo-classical design ethos has now arrived. These chairs have guilloche (spiral carved decoration) and fluted tapering legs. Such delicate constructions are not suited to large heavy Georgian country squires!

Below: Mahogany chairs in the Gothic style, circa 1775. The supports for the arms are called 'clasped' columns. The Georgian Gothic style lasted from the middle years of the 18th century on into the Victorian period and didn't really end until World War I. At various times in that period of about 150 years, designers looked over their shoulders to the imagined golden age of the Middle Ages and used medieval-type ornaments.

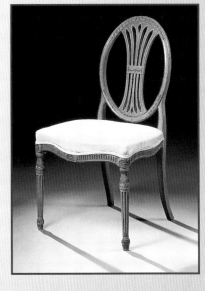

Right: A painted beech side-chair in the manner of John Linnell, circa 1775: a neo-classical chair with painted decoration. The Adam brothers made painted decoration acceptable.

Below: A pair of painted beech chairs in the manner of George Seddon, circa 1800. These chairs are barely neo-classical. They are moving on towards Regency which was only 11 years away. The use of ebonizing gives the chairs a slightly mysterious Oriental quality, and provides a perfect ground for the gilded leaves and painted flower decoration. Form has finally become more important than function.

Above: Mahogany chairs, circa 1775. These are relatively simple, inexpensive chairs to make, but they still have a touch of neo-classical decoration in the palm-like ends to the splats and the disc medallions in the middle of the splats.

Above: Mahogany armchairs, circa 1780. These have paterae and bell-flower carving. They look French, but are in fact English.

We now come to the end of the most important century in the history of British furniture. Britain was at war with Revolutionary France. In the 18th century massive changes had taken place in the design world, the industrial world and in the political world.

Let us start in the dining room – the older Georgians would have approved of this location!

Above: This sideboard of classical Georgian design is 5ft (1525mm) wide and was made around 1795 from mahogany with rosewood cross-banding. It is a small, well-proportioned piece made in a style that is very fashionable to this day.

Right: This is a plate carrier, made in mahogany and brass-bound, dating from about 1790. Rarely seen these days, it was used by the serving staff to carry plates from the scullery to the dining room. This model has an open edge but a bucket type was also made. The problem of keeping food warm or drinks cold, produced a variety of ingenious solutions. Plate-warmers with hot-water jackets were made, as were coolers which contained ice. In both cases the water tended to leak over the furniture, giving the furniture restorer plenty to do.

Below: A mahogany drum table, 24in (610mm) wide, circa 1795. I have included it because it shows the downswept legs – a style of leg in which appearance is more important than strength. The problem of short grain which leads to snapped-off components was completely ignored between 1770 and 1840. Here is a bold generalization: if a piece of English furniture looks structurally weak it was probably made in the last years of the 18th or the first years of the 19th centuries!

Above: A mahogany dining table made in the last five years of the 18th century. It is very simple with tapering legs, decorated with ebony and boxwood lines.

Below: Another form of table that became popular at this time was the pedestal table. This type is a breakfast table, circa 1795. There is scope for confusion here! The term 'breakfast table' was first used by Chippendale in the Directory (1762). However, the piece that Chippendale illustrates under this name consists of a two-flap table with shelves or cupboards underneath; this type is rarely seen these days. Much more common are rectangular tables raised on pedestals. From the end of the 18th century, eating became less formal and more intimate. Small tables were easier to set, and so a fashion developed for taking meals in a smaller room at a smaller table. The smaller room was called the 'breakfast room'.

Below: Now we move firmly into the satinwood period with a needlework table in West Indian satinwood, 1ft 7in (485mm) wide, circa 1790. The top is cross-banded in kingwood and the slender tapering legs have ebony arris lines.

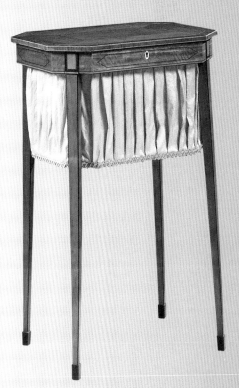

Above: A West Indian satinwood side cabinet, circa 1795. The central door is glazed and it would be more likely to contain porcelain than books. Notice that although it has the straight lines and also the neo-classical urn designs of the better pieces from the period, it still appears awkwardly proportioned, and badly veneered: not everything Georgian was good. However, the next piece brings us back up to standard.

Left: A 2ft 9in (840mm) wide West Indian satinwood secretaire bookcase with purpleheart banding. This has Georgian 'Gothick' lancet glazing, with an elegant line and banded decoration. Compare this to the last item and you can see the importance of proportion in design. Each element of the design is balanced within its particular space and also within the entire piece.

Above: A cabinet with a secretaire drawer, cupboards below and two small brass galleried bookshelves above. It was made around 1795, is 2ft 6in (760mm) wide and is veneered in West Indian satinwood and burr yew.

Below: Sofa table in West Indian satinwood. With the Pembroke table, this is a standard item in any re-creation of a late-Georgian room setting. These tables often stood behind a sofa, hence the name we now use. The tops are prone to warping and shrinking. The rule joints at the ends can be pulled inwards by shrinkage of the centre section, so the leaves do not hang vertically and the table is said to be 'flying'. The drawers may open on one side only, or one on each side, with false drawer fronts opposite. Beware of later 'knock-ups', using cheval mirror supports as legs: you can spot these by the mysterious patches in the underframe. In this example the twin columns of the legs come down to yoke supports with brass castors.

Above: A rosewood and West Indian satinwood bonheur-du-jour after a design by Hepplewhite. The drawer is pulled partly out and the flap above it is opened and rests on the drawer. The last three items were all made using the simple, often straight, lines that typified the late 18th century.

Above: After satinwood came rosewood. This was not the rosewood that we know today, but Rio rosewood, Dalbergia nigra, the felling of which is now illegal. This side table is veneered in rosewood, with a marble top and gilded decoration. It was made in 1810 and from a design point of view there are hardly any 18th-century elements in it. The most significant part of the design is the spiral baluster turning with gilded flutes – these are 19th-century elements which we will see again and again.

Above: This is a mahogany, satinwood and gilt-brass-mounted writing cabinet, probably made by Seddon, Sons and Shackleton, London. The partnership included George Seddon's sons and son-in-law. Although made in the last five years of the 18th century, this piece really looks as though it was made in the first years of the following century. The structure is massive – it is solid with almost engineered precision and complexity. The slide has a sloping writing surface with a brass-ratchet support. Slides, cylinders and sloping writing surfaces had been made for many years, but this example has everything compressed into a small space, and the brass pieces finely machined. The makers and purchasers of this piece wanted something that opened and closed like an engineered apparatus.

Above: Other exotic woods were used in the 19th century. One of these was calamander. This is a writing table made circa 1810. It has a gallery, but could have been used in the positions of centre table, sofa table, or writing table – in other words, in the middle of the room, behind the sofa, against a wall or under a window. A distinctive feature of early 19th-century furniture was the use of mercury-gilded brass decoration.

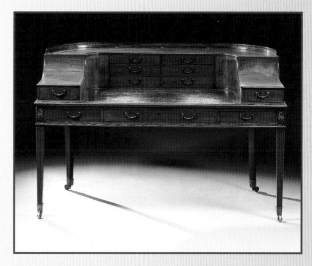

Above: A Carlton House desk from about 1790. This languid piece of furniture is as much of a contrast to the preceding item as one could get. Although George IV ruled until 1830, in furniture terms the 'Georgian' period ended when 'Regency' started. George, Prince of Wales was made Regent in 1811, but he was having a significant effect on fashion 20 years before that. A table of this model was reputedly made for the Prince of Wales's London residence, Carlton House, in 1790. At this stage the Prince Regent was commissioning furniture in the traditional Georgian style. By 1811 the new 'Regency' style had taken root.

ENGLAND 1810 – 1820

In political terms the Regency began in 1811 and ended in 1820 when George III died and his son, the Prince Regent, ascended the throne and became George IV. However the influence of the Prince Regent on art and fashion had begun over 20 years earlier as shown by the Carlton House desk shown in the previous section.

Above: We begin with a pair of mahogany card tables, made circa 1810. They have D-shaped tops, a simple frieze with a single bead enclosing an empty panel, and tapering, reeded legs. The empty panel was a reaction to over-decoration, the new belief being that if a piece was well proportioned, the attractive form of the object was sufficient in itself. These are not examples of Grand Furniture, but simple, classically based designs, easily produced for the new middle classes. The audience for the furniture-makers was changing. A new century, the end of the Napoleonic Wars and success in industry, produced patrons who were not drawn from the aristocracy. Of course the upper classes still commissioned furniture, but the makers had to satisfy a demand from further down the social scale as well.

Right: Next, a pair of small tripod tables, circa 1810. These have rosewood tops with brass edges and are raised on gilded and ebonized pillars. They are slightly rarer than the previous card tables, but are still furniture that was made for general consumption, not as one-off commissions for the Great Houses. As we enter the 19th century it is noticeable that more ordinary furniture was being made. In the 18th century, cabinetmakers had a small clientele, but by the start of the 19th century there were many more people able to purchase fashionable furniture and thus a greater market for small batch production. Another change was that machining processes had now worked their way into cabinetmaking. Thomas Hope complained about 'the entire substitution of machinery to manual labour' in his Household Furniture, **published in 1807.**

Below: A double-sided mahogany writing table, circa 1810. This is a pattern from which many hundreds were made. It is simple, easily manufactured and of good classical proportions.

Below and bottom: Not only were Nelson's victories influential in altering design, but they were actually recorded in commemorative items of furniture and ceramics. This chest of drawers dates from about 1806. The inset photograph shows a close-up of one of the brass handles. In the centre is a pyramid-like triangular tablet with the words 'Sacred to Nelson' flanked by two cannon and a trophy of arms with the word 'Trafalgar' below, all of this within a Greek key border. This is a pressed brass backplate, not a casting. The process of pressing brass had become commonplace by the start of the 19th century.

Below: A burr oak library table with ebonized enrichments. This piece is after a design by Charles Tatham, circa 1799, Thomas Hope, circa 1807, and George Smith, circa 1808. Each designer adapted and revised his predecessor's drawings. Variety in designs was becoming more commonplace. The Battle of the Nile (1798), the first of Nelson's victories, brought to everyday England the fabled symbols of the East: the sphinx, the chimera (wings of an eagle, head of a lion and tail of a serpent), camels, pyramids and palms. Greek motifs such as the lyre and the anthemion (honeysuckle) were popular. This trend had started in about 1795, but it wasn't until the middle and late Regency period that the Greek revival and the other 'concept' designs such as Chinese or Gothic became widespread.

Left and below: Two visually quite dissimilar sideboards that were both made in about 1815. The increased publication of design books and the expansion in workshops as well as clients during the Regency period made for a greater variety of furniture shapes, some in later years becoming quite extravagant. Both these sideboards are in mahogany. The one at left is of standard Georgian form, bow-fronted, central drawer flanked by pairs of real or false drawers. But the legs are Egyptian with Sphinx mask capitals. The one below shows a new design, the recessed centre. This was influenced by the massive masonry of the newly discovered Egyptian ruins but also harked back to the days when large pedestals flanked the central surface of the sideboard. The Regency was almost a time of 'anything goes', and some contemporary commentators lamented the passing of good taste.

Below: A rosewood bonheur-du-jour, circa 1815. It has some new and very Regency features such as the square section of most of the timbers, cabriole supports rather like a console table, and gilded brass spheres as feet. The gilt brass galleries and leaf ornaments are neo-classically derived but are not new, as these shapes had been used throughout the 17th and 18th centuries. What is new about this model – illustrated in one of the design books and then copied many times – is the quality of the cabinetwork, the mounts and the finish. Many French craftsmen fled to Britain during the wars and brought with them metal-casting skills and French polish. The high-gloss surface, which enhanced the figure of the wood, began to be used in Britain.

Right: Another new item of furniture to emerge at this time was the revolving bookcase. Like this one, they are usually in mahogany and have the older Georgian proportions in order to carry the weight of books. What makes them possible is a steel mechanism below the bottom shelf with concealed rollers taking the weight as the superstructure is revolved.

Above: If a piece of furniture looks structurally weak it was probably made at the end of the 18th or at the beginning of the 19th century. Here is such an item: a rosewood sofa table, circa 1815. The piece is well made, the figure in the veneer is wonderful, the neo-classical scrolls are well proportioned, but the legs and the U-shaped support are waiting to break!

Above: A mahogany side cabinet, circa 1820. At first glance this looks 18th-century, but the spiral pilasters and the use of brass grilles and pleated panels give it away. The feet are gilt metal, which is another sign of 19th-century origin.

Above and below: These two examples are of pieces that were clearly 'one-offs'. The library table and pair of marble-topped cabinets are from a suite of furniture made by John Wellsman for Creely Park in Devon, England in 1820. They are rosewood and brass, inlaid in the typical high Regency fashion. The beaded mouldings and deeply carved paw feet on both are typical of the period, as is the sturdy triangular-section concave pillar and the concave platform base on the table.

Above: A wonderful George IV bookcase in rosewood, circa 1820. This piece of furniture is made more to show off the timbers and the inlaid classical figures than to hold books, although in fact the figures are inlaid onto door panels with shelves behind. Note the main early 19th-century features: straight blocks of timber, large expanses of very well figured rosewood, beaded mouldings, anthemion inlay to the stiles, very simple architectural pediment, and heavy plinth.

This was a period influenced by three sovereigns. First came George IV, who was Regent from 1811 to 1820, then King from 1820 to 1830. Second came the brief reign of William IV, 1830 to 1837. He was George IV's brother and Victoria's uncle. Finally, Queen Victoria began her long reign in 1837, which continued until 1901.

Above: A cellarette, 36in (914mm) wide, early 19th century. This has fashionable Regency ornaments: lotus leaves, reeding, beading and festoons, all on beautifully figured mahogany.

Right: A rosewood and brass-inlaid card table, circa 1820. A modest amount of brass decoration, but a rather clumpy column.

Left: A rosewood davenport, circa 1820. The first recorded davenport was made by Gillows for a Captain Davenport. They come with various contrivances – rising stationery compartments, sliding tops – but are always of the same general shape as shown here.

Below: A rosewood games table attributed to Gillows, circa 1820. The beautifully proportioned supports and good cabinetwork, together with a drawing of a similar table by Gillows, support the attribution. The slide is veneered to match the top on one side and has a chess board on the other. Below is a backgammon well.

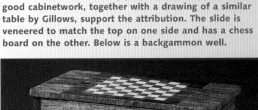

Below: A mahogany and rosewood bookcase, circa 1822. This is close to a design by **Richard Brown,** in The Rudiments of Drawing Cabinet and Upholstery Furniture, **1822. This is** an example of a late design and has an over-emphasis on turned supports. There is no need for the free-standing columns – visually they conflict with the solidity of the cupboards that they enclose.

Below: A mahogany double-sided writing table, circa 1820. This is not as graceful as earlier examples. There are too many ring turnings and the knees above the splayed legs are not elegant; also, the lower legs look a little squashed.

Left: A mahogany hat-and-coat stand, circa 1820.

Above: A rosewood side-cabinet with marble top, circa 1820. This is nicely proportioned and the gadrooned feet are kept inside the line of the carcass. Behind the grilles are false book-spines.

Above: A rosewood secretaire bookcase, circa 1825. In this example the columns have been brought inside the outline of the cabinet, but even so they still look uncomfortable, as do the glazing bars.

Above: A mahogany dressing table, circa 1820. An elegant table, not over-decorated, and in the manner of Gillows.

Above: A mahogany three-pedestal dining-table, circa 1820. It is simple and solid. Similar pieces are still made today.

Right: A mahogany patent-action dining-table, circa 1820. A far less robust table, but one which takes up less space. The supports concertina inwards as the ends are pushed together, and the result is that an 11ft (3.35m) table is reduced to 5ft (1.52m) square. The search for new ideas produced all sorts of odd patented pieces of furniture.

A pollard oak breakfast-table, circa 1820. The desire for originality has produced very unconventional feet. The cross-banding is in coromandel.

A rosewood games table, circa 1820. Another example with a sliding top. Not as elegantly proportioned as the Gillows example, but nicely illustrating the taste for unusual supports.

Above: A rosewood sofa table, circa 1825. The supports are a little ungainly, but serve their purpose.

A pair of mahogany wine-coolers, circa 1820. These are standard Regency form, very plain, but very nice.

Above: A mahogany dining table, circa 1825. Being in the manner of Gillows, this is more attractive than the earlier mahogany patent-action dining table on the previous page – I would expect the mechanism to work better, as well.

Left: A pair of rosewood tables, circa 1825. These are excellent quality tables, also in the manner of Gillows. These really are at the top end of the market, with such crisp, well-proportioned carving.

RELEVANT DATES

1805	Battle of Trafalgar
1807	Slave trade abolished in the British Empire
1811	Prince George assumes the role of Regent
1815	Battle of Waterloo
1820	George IV ascends throne
1824	Byron, the poet, dies while fighting for Greek freedom
1830	William IV ascends throne; first passenger steam railways
1832	Reform Bill extends vote to middle classes
1833	Factory Act bans children under nine from employment in factories
1834	Tolpuddle Martyrs attempt to form first Trade Union
1836	Chartist movement demands vote for all adult males
1837	Victoria ascends throne

ENGLAND 1830 – 1837

In this section we continue to look at furniture from the time of George IV, George's brother William IV and William's niece Queen Victoria, whose long and eventful reign began in 1837 and lasted until the beginning of the 20th century.

Left: A mahogany open bookcase, circa 1825. Classic design, nice and simple with not over-carved feet.

Right: A pollard oak, brass-inlaid pedestal desk, circa 1825. This is a good solid desk with attractive inlay and no unnecessary ornament. The interior has a central-locking mechanism. It is attributed to the royal cabinetmakers Morel and Seddon.

Below: A rosewood, parcel-gilt and marble-inlaid games table, circa 1825: a splendid specimen with top and supports that are graceful, strong and visually effective.

Below: Here is another 'imaginary Gothic' table, circa 1830.

Above: Throughout the 19th century various examples of Gothic Revival furniture were made. This fashion was encouraged by Sir Walter Scott's novels. The furniture produced varied in quality and accuracy. Given that bookcases were not made in Gothic times, this is a good-quality interpretation of what a 'Gothic' cabinetmaker might have made, circa 1830.

Above: A glimpse inside the mahogany dumbwaiter.

Below: This is a mahogany dumbwaiter, circa 1840. The top is formed from three boards that are linked by cords and counter-weighted. When closed the piece looks like an ordinary side-table; when opened the shelves give three times the space of a serving table.

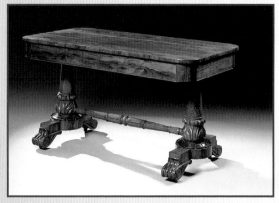

Above: This is a William IV rosewood library-table, circa 1835. The style is still based on Regency designs, but just a little less detail was put into the carving.

Above: This is a very nice mahogany sideboard with book-matched veneers, dating from about 1835. The Regency reeding is still present, as are the 'legs outside the carcass'. The carving is very crisp and is of the same quality as the veneering, but the design has a certain heaviness about it which is associated with William IV furniture.

Above: A marble-topped table with rosewood base, 3ft 6in (1067mm) wide, circa 1835. The Regency features of feet, scrolls, concave platform base, gadrooning and fluting are all very slightly too 'heavy', which is why it is attributed to the reign of William IV.

Above: A circular extending dining-table by Robert Jupe, circa 1835. The extension pieces can be seen in the picture – these are lifted out and the segments pushed inwards to make a smaller circle.

Above: Now here is a heavy piece of furniture! The top is heavy, the column is heavy and the feet are heavy – all characteristic of the William IV period. It is a library table, circa 1835, with concealed drawers in the frieze.

Above: Another library table, good and solid. This was made just as Victoria was coming to the throne, and the Victorians would have approved of the solid four-square mahogany construction.

Above: This is a mahogany William IV breakfast table – lots of carving, but it's rather flat and 'dead'. Circa 1835.

Above: Here is a nice mahogany side-table, circa 1835. It is rather on the heavy side, but has good classical proportions. It could well have stood in the entrance hall of a country house.

Above: The early 19th-century fashion for brass inlay reached a climax in the 1830s. This centre table, circa 1835, in the manner of leading London cabinetmakers Town and Emanuel, is typical in its over-decorated surfaces, lacking in proportion and design flair.

Above: This three-tier dumbwaiter trolley, circa 1840, has less panache than that shown on page 121. The counter-balanced mechanisms are gone, as is the attempt at decoration on the supports. This really is the precursor of the tea trolley. Fine furniture had entered the mass-produced age.

Right: This is a William IV version of a davenport, circa 1835. In this version, 15 years later than the one on page 117, the crispness of line has gone. The quality of enrichments, carcass construction and veneering is much lower. This is not to say that all mid 19th-century furniture is of poorer quality than its forebears, but it was often the case that popular furniture was cheaper in construction than the originals. This is still true today.

CONTINENTAL
1800 – 1810

Above: I start with an Italian piece that dates from the last decade of the 18th century. This is a bureau cabinet by F. Abbiati, 4ft 8in (1420mm) high and 3ft 2in (965mm) wide. This splendid pen-engraved cabinet is of architectonic form (design related to the principles of architecture) with one long and two short sprung drawers above a central fall with a single deep drawer below. All the motifs are taken from antiquity and include Ceres, Jove, Minerva, Neptune and Hercules. I include it in this section because, although it is obviously based on classical influences, it also displays one of the major characteristics of 19th-century furniture – excess. This will become more apparent later in the century but, as a general rule, if you get the feeling that the artist didn't know where to stop, the object is likely to be 19th-century.

Europe was at war. The first decade of the 19th century was not a good time for designers and makers. Imagine how the French cabinetmakers must have felt when their clientele, the aristocracy, virtually ceased to exist. Not only had the clients been decimated, so had the guilds. The French Revolution, in its eagerness for universal enfranchisement, rendered illegal the guilds, which had enforced stringent rules for the making of furniture. It was no longer legally necessary to serve an apprenticeship, and be elected *maître*, before one could sell one's work.

RELEVANT DATES

1799	Napoleon sets up Consulate to rule France
1800	French defeat Austrians. Italian scientist Volta makes first electric battery
1801	Treaty of Lunéville gives France most of Italy
1804	Bonaparte created Emperor. Empire period begins. First steam locomotive built by Trevithick in England
1805	Battle of Trafalgar
1806	Prussia defeated by French
1808	French occupy Spain

An Italian commode from the first part of the 19th century. Contrary to what I said about the Italian bureau cabinet, I would not call this over-decorated. One of the ways in which such pieces would be assessed is to note that the decoration occupies a large amount of the surface area; that fact, together with constructional details, such as timber preparation, type of joints and so on, would lead to the conclusion that the items were 19th-century. In such an assessment the knowledge of the history of layout and of the motifs depicted is the backdrop against which a dating decision is taken. That is why drawing from real objects is such a vital part of the study of furniture.

Below: An Italian mahogany commode, circa 1805. This is a total change from the previous two illustrations. It is similar to the French Empire style. At this time Napoleon had briefly occupied Rome and no doubt the Italian makers conformed to the current fashions. It is rather difficult to be precise in attempting to relate politics to design because the early 19th century was a time of such frequent change. For example The Directoire (which ruled France), after which was named the Directoire style, lasted only from 1795 to 1799. Then The Consulate started and lasted until 1804, when The Empire was declared. It was a very complex time for designers, and for historians.

Below: Returning to furniture we move into Revolutionary France. This secrétaire à abattant illustrates how much fashions have changed. This example, made circa 1800 in the Empire style, shows the simple gilt-brass classically based ornament that was acceptable during the 'Empire' period. Napoleon was a military man. He cared nothing for flowing decoration based upon nature – he wanted simple forms based upon previous great empires – those of Rome, Greece and Egypt. To own beauty as well as wealth was to fall under the suspicion of being an aristocrat.

The next piece shows how much the French Revolution affected such non-political activities as furniture-making. This is another secrétaire à abattant, from circa 1800. This time the timber used is elm, which has no association with the Anción Regime. This maker may have been afraid that the use of mahogany indicated too close an association with aristocracy. The motifs are clearly revolutionary: arrows and the Jacobin fasces.

Above: Next we have an Empire mahogany commode, circa 1805. The piece relies for its decoration on the veneer selection and the bronzes. The new clients of the French cabinetmakers soon found that mahogany looked better than elm. The mounts on the drawer are classically derived; those on the pilasters are based on Egyptian motifs. Egypt was being 'rediscovered' at about this time, and Egyptian motifs appeared on both French and British furniture.

A pair of Directoire mahogany meubles d'appui, circa 1800; the mounts are later. Meubles d'appui are low storage cupboards for placement against a wall. There is little that one can say about these cupboards other than that they have an almost military simplicity. It is ironic that the century began with simple furniture which was born out of the Revolution and subsequently became plagued with complex over-decorated furniture, born out of excess and over-indulgence.

Below: An Empire cheval mirror in mahogany, circa 1810. The term 'cheval' refers to the fact that the large mirror (large, flat glass was a relatively new development) is supported on a strong frame, as a horse supports its rider. The gilt bronze mounts include flaming torches and laurel wreaths, both motifs with classical Roman associations.

Above: The preceding five pieces have all been very plain in appearance. This was the effect the French revolution had on design. By 1810, the worst period for persecution had passed and designers were slightly less restricted. Here is a mahogany commode from around that date. The bulbous feet and columns above gave the maker a chance to try out different decorative techniques. Notice that he has stayed away from anything resembling rococo gilt bronze decoration. The mounts are in shapes that the maker believed would have appeared familiar to a Roman senator or to an Egyptian courtier.

Above: Finally, for this section of French Revolutionary furniture, here is quite a plain mahogany side table made in the early 19th century. The ruthless avoidance of any decoration shows how simple the revolutionary furniture had to be. In fact, it is almost impossible to date this piece because it has practically no design features at all.

Below: Napoleon was famous for his administration as well as his feats on the battlefield. He spent a lot of time reading and writing reports and orders. Desks were important features of Napoleonic life. However, as this bureau plat illustrates, the desk had to be functional and not wildly decorated with decadent motifs like those of the previous regime.

Above: While we are in the eastern part of Europe we must not forget another, much older, empire – that of Russia. Peter the Great had modernised Russia at the start of the 18th century and this process continued throughout the century. The architecture of St. Petersburg was modelled on the French styles. Russian furniture makers also used French designs as models. Here is a Russian mahogany commode, with three short and two long drawers, circa 1810.

Above: Before we leave this decade, let us look farther afield. Here is a Baltic armoire, circa 1800. The timber is mahogany, the shape is breakfront, but the basic form is Greco-Roman. The Baltic countries, with their sailing and trading traditions, were receptive to new design ideas from elsewhere in Europe.

CONTINENTAL
1810 – 1820

During the Empire period French cabinetmakers were subdued, as were many other craftsmen. The quieter the life, the less likely you were to draw attention to yourself, which at this turbulent time could have proved dangerous.

Left: We start with a mahogany cabinet, which typifies the artistic reticence which characterized the period. The top is black marble, the mounts are gilt metal and classical in origin. The whole piece is subdued, almost boring.

Right: The guéridon table, circa 1815, is a curious piece. The top is marble, the column is bronze and only the base is mahogany. I find it hard to believe that this was part of the design tradition that led Europe.

Above: Slightly more exciting, but still relying for decorative effect upon gilt-metal mounts placed onto a plain carcass, is this secrétaire à abattant, circa 1815. It is only 2ft 2in (660mm) wide and perhaps intended for use in a bedroom. At first glance it looks rather like a dressing table in that it has a mirrored fall; however, the interior reveals that it is a piece of writing furniture.

Above: By the time that this mahogany cupboard emerged – circa 1820 – boldness was starting to creep back into the artistic community. The form of this piece is very simple, but the allegory in the mounts is sophisticated. The gilt bronze figure is Nike, Greek goddess of victory, and the sides are adorned with laurel wreaths, also associated with victory. At this time Greece was striving for independence and French pride was recovering following the ravages of the recent wars (and national defeat). As a nation the French rejected all images associated with revolution and restored a King – Louis XVIII. The use of the image of Nike may relate to any of these situations. Whatever the case, this maker was obviously no longer subdued by fear, and art and classical literature were being restored to the French nation.

Above and below: Both of these items of early 'office' furniture come from the Restoration period, when the French royal family was returned to the throne. They are both rather ponderous and very functional. Their drawers are faced with green gilt-tooled leather.

Above: Note the very subdued decoration on this burr-walnut circular centre-table, circa 1815, stamped 'Jacob'. The piece is elegant, but its clearly neutral tone suggests that neither the maker nor the purchaser had any clearly defined political allegiances.

Left: By around 1810 the French Empire style had spread throughout Europe and had become interpreted as rather severe and massive, with little ornament. You could easily mistake this mahogany and burr-walnut bureau cabinet for art deco, when in fact it was made 120 years earlier in about 1810. The design is faintly classical in that it has a stepped top and Nubian terms at the sides of the fall. The style is called Biedermeier, after a satirical newspaper character called Papa Biedermeier, who was famous for expressing simple, no-nonsense political opinions.

In a similar vein the early furniture was lightly classical, often using light-coloured woods like birch, cherry, maple and ash, and devoid of excessive ornament. At around this time, European furniture-making was changing. Machines made production easier, but stifled the relationship between draughtsman/designer and craftsman. In the past the craftsman had often been the draughtsman/designer. And the rise of the middle classes in Europe led to a demand for furniture that was easy on the eye, easy on the intellect and easy on the pocket. Factories met that demand, styles became watered down, and dealers no longer cared how objects looked, just as long as they sold.

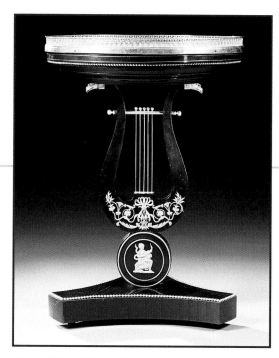

Above: This guéridon table on an ebony-veneered lyre support and platform base is more inspiring. This 1820s piece features well-made mounts, unlike the previous piece. The use of double-knife-cut ebony veneer indicates a piece of some quality, even though some people may feel that the lyre, medallion and concave base do not sit well as a visual ensemble.

Left: An Austrian walnut secrétaire à abattant, circa 1820, is an example of the way in which styles bounced around Europe in the 19th century. The fall has been pen-engraved with a classical scene. Pen engraving of this rather maudlin romantic sort was popular in the middle and last quarter of the century in Britain. In central Europe it was popular in the first quarter of the century. You will see that despite the ebonized columns, the feet and the gilt-brass mounts, this item has little in common with the well-made, well-designed Empire furniture that inspired it.

Right: Moving swiftly over the Alps for a brief visit to Italy, here are a mirror and console table, circa 1820, both in mahogany. Again the Empire style is retained, but with much more elegance.

Above: Our final piece from the old Austro-Hungarian Empire is a curious tripod table with very pretty verre-églomisé top and strangely squashed legs. Verre églomisé is glass decorated on the underside with engraved gold-leaf, which, in turn, is backed by another layer of either glass, paint or varnish. The supports have an attractive sweep to them, but it looks as though the maker went just about as far as he could with curved elements, without having access to modern laminating techniques.

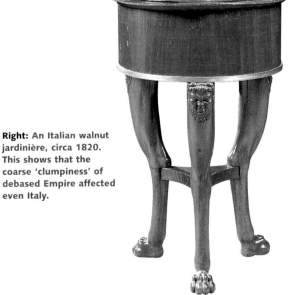

Right: An Italian walnut jardinière, circa 1820. This shows that the coarse 'clumpiness' of debased Empire affected even Italy.

RELEVANT DATES

1812	Napoleon invades Russia and is then forced to retreat. Charles Dickens born
1813	French defeated by Austrian, Russian and Prussian armies, and driven out of Spain by Wellington
1814	Napoleon abdicates and is exiled to Elba. Restoration of Louis XVIII, brother of the executed Louis XVI. Restoration period begins
1815	Napoleon escapes from Elba and seizes power in France again. Later in the year he is crushed at Waterloo and exiled to St Helena. End of First French Empire in a political sense
1819	Industrial Exhibition in Louvre: 'Supremacy of technique to the detriment of art'
1820	Revolts in Spain, Portugal and Italy
1821	Napoleon dies on St Helena
1821	Greek War of Independence against Turkey
1823	Spanish revolution crushed
1824	Accession of Charles X (brother to Louis XVI and Louis XVIII) in France
1827	Treaty of London guarantees Greek independence
1830	July Revolution in Paris: Charles X overthrown Louis-Philippe (descendant of Louis XIII), 'The Citizen King', ascends

CONTINENTAL
1820 – 1830

Left: The Moorish influence is evident in this Spanish table-top in calamander, fruitwood, brass and copper, circa 1820. The European influence in this piece is confined to the supports (which are not visible in the photograph). The base has a baluster stem with traditional splayed legs, gilt-bronze sabots and brass castors.

Right: The Russian and Baltic countries favoured rich mahogany-veneered curves, as seen in this Empire-style brass and inlaid-mahogany wine-cooler from the Baltic, circa 1815. The stylized double-winged crests bear an obvious affinity with the heraldic arms of Eastern Europe.

Above: We now move to Italy to look at a cherrywood pedestal desk, circa 1820. It has Egyptian heads to the term figures, but also shield-shaped escutcheons, which are a late 18th-century English feature.

Above: We leave Italy with a fleeting glimpse of a cherry dining table, circa 1830. The supports are pretty unbelievable, as is the whole construction – the top pulls out to accept two extra leaves, to which four detachable tapering legs are screwed on at the corners.

Above: A detail shot of a walnut and cypresswood secrétaire à abattant by A. Fantastici, circa 1830. The ebonized terms and sea-horses are all carved. This piece of grand furniture, which was made for the Villa del Pavone, is an example of what was possible if one left mass production behind and returned to properly designed and made furniture.

Above: Back to France and a mahogany Restoration desk, circa 1825. It has the heavy, ungainly Empire-derived column legs with gilt-bronze capitals.

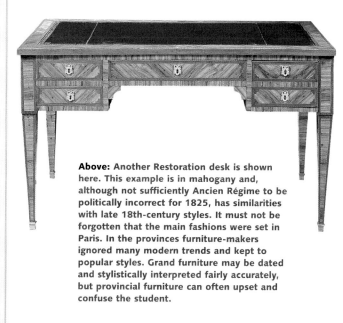

Above: Another Restoration desk is shown here. This example is in mahogany and, although not sufficiently Ancien Régime to be politically incorrect for 1825, has similarities with late 18th-century styles. It must not be forgotten that the main fashions were set in Paris. In the provinces furniture-makers ignored many modern trends and kept to popular styles. Grand furniture may be dated and stylistically interpreted fairly accurately, but provincial furniture can often upset and confuse the student.

Above: This Charles X burr-walnut dressing table, circa 1830, has column legs and is similar to the Restoration desk, but is altogether better proportioned.

Below: A simple wash-stand, circa 1820, in mahogany with a grey marble top, cut to receive a metal bowl. It bears the label 'Jacob Desmalter & Compagnie', one of the most fashionable cabinetmakers in Paris.

Above: A Charles X burr-walnut gilt-mounted dressing-table, circa 1830, 36in (914mm) wide, which, being subdued and not over-decorated, is characteristic of its era. In general, French cabinetmakers were rather quiet in the period leading up to the Second Empire which began in 1848. Instead, interest centred on the Exhibitions which were opportunities to display technical advancements such as carving machines, veneer cutters and other mechanized processes, rather than grand furniture. Grand pieces were made, but the buying public wanted less expensive, more mediocre items. The hinged lid of the table rises to reveal a mirrored interior with divided compartments. 18th-century design was based upon principles that could be, and were, written down, and which had a certain logic. That was not the case in the 19th century and it was the middle classes who were responsible for this being so. They didn't want the responsibility of understanding principles – they wanted a design ethos that was easy on the intellect.

Below: Belgian furniture is very well made and has a neatness about it. This Belgian dining table, circa 1830, splits in the middle and accepts an extra leaf.

Above: Before we leave this decade I have two more interesting illustrations – the first being a curved Karelian birch bookcase, circa 1830, which is probably Baltic in origin as this timber was very popular in Russia and Scandinavia. This must have been a one-off for a curved room, but I am sure that a flat bookcase from the same workshop would have had a similar elevation. The curved wall was a popular early 19th-century feature and curved furniture was made to fit it.

Below: Finally, a very fine giltwood centre-table by K.F. Schinkel, circa 1830. This table is one of a pair made for a German palace in the High German Greek revival style. Most German furniture of this decade was in a watered-down Empire (subsequently called Biedermeier) style. This watering-down of styles applied, with the exception of Grand Furniture for noble houses or exhibitions, throughout Europe in the first three decades of the 19th century; money, rather than taste, was controlling what was made. The increased volume of output, brought about by the use of mass production, which matched the demand from the new middle-classes, meant that, in the chase for increased sales, manufacturers were willing to try anything. The result was the end of purity of style.

Above: A centre-table with Belgian marble top, circa 1830. This has the much more common 19th-century bulbous faceted column and engraved line decoration. Both characteristics are very easily undertaken in mass production. There are records of early 19th-century furniture factories employing 300 workers. That certainly was 'mass' production.

CHAPTER

FOUR

Chairs and the 19th Century

ENGLISH CHAIRS
1800 – 1840 PART I

There is so much variety in chair design that the subject needs to be considered in five parts. Part I will deal with standard models, Part II with less common variations, Part III with oddities, Part IV with upholstered chairs and the final section, Part V, with settees.

Above and right: This chair is of the standard Regency design, much copied even today. One of the reasons that they are so copied is that they are very simple. The examples shown are made of mahogany, circa 1810, with reeded frames and drop-in seats. Make sure the correct seat goes in the correct frame, because sizes can vary. A seat that is too wide can break the joints when weight is put upon it and in this design there is very little strength in the joints holding the left-hand side of the chair to the right-hand side.

SOVEREIGNS

George III	1760–1820
George IV	(Regent 1811–1820, King 1820–1830)
William IV	1830–1837 (brother to George IV and uncle to Victoria)
Victoria	1837–1901

Below: The twisted rope decoration on the crest rail is sometimes called 'cabling', and is suggested to be emblematic of British naval activities, especially Nelson's victories. Sometimes such chairs are called 'Trafalgar' chairs. This example is in simulated rosewood – therefore not very good quality – and is rather late, circa 1815. The over-decoration of the central clasp-shaped splat with carving and brass rosettes confirms this.

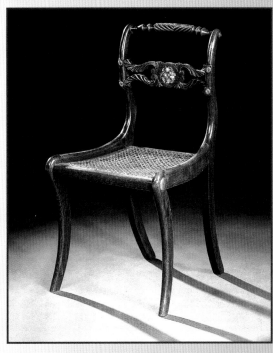

Above: Here is another example of the standard Regency design, in mahogany, circa 1810. These have the front seat rail slightly lower in the knee to try to give more strength, but this does make them look slightly less attractive. There is always a compromise between strength and design. The upholstery fabric is known as Regency stripe.

Below: This is the armchair from a set of 12 Regency chairs, which are top-of-the-range except that they are not in rosewood, but mahogany. They have double sabre legs, rope decoration, brass inlay and low relief engraved design, circa 1815. The arms may not fit under a dining table.

Left: This Regency chair is in simulated rosewood, circa 1815. It is, in fact, beech. The seat is caned, with a squab cushion on top. The wide panel of the back splat is actually rosewood, so watch out for part graining, part real timber!

Left: Here are another two from a set of eight mahogany chairs, circa 1815. In this style the crest rail often comes loose, due to handling, and spins around in its sockets. Good gluing or a tiny dowel made on a draw plate will act as a key to prevent this. Don't use panel pins, though – future restorers don't want to suddenly find bits of metal where there need only be timber.

Above: These are two from a set of ten mahogany dining chairs, circa 1820. They have spiral reeding or 'rope' decoration on the legs. The little wooden spheres, held between the horizontal splats, were an early 19th-century ornamental device.

Left: A good, solid, straightforward mahogany George IV armchair. These were sometimes called 'carver' chairs because they were placed at the head of the table. In this case that would be rather difficult, because the arms come down to the top of the front legs and might hit the table top. True carvers should really have the arms attached halfway along the side seat rail.

Above: These are standard George IV mahogany dining chairs, circa 1830. They still have the deep, solid crest rail, which is a classical touch, but are raised on sturdy turned and reeded supports. In later years these supports became more massive and rather ungainly.

Left: This is a slightly later version of the Gillows chairs, but by a very different maker. Although the curve of the back is reminiscent of classical designs, the back has become squat and ungraceful. These characteristics are often associated with William IV furniture. Top-notch makers like Gillows had their cheaper, second- and third-division imitators.

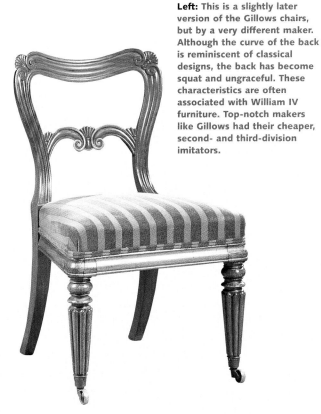

Above: This set of George IV mahogany dining chairs was made in the manner of Gillows. They are a complete reaction to the flimsy chairs of the late 18th and early 19th centuries. They are very fine quality and are stamped with the journeymen's initials 'E.L.' and 'H.C.'

Above: These are two from a long set of 21 dining chairs. They are mahogany and early Victorian, circa 1840. There is little to associate these chairs with the classical designs of the Regency. Although the back is elegant and restrained, it is hardly classically derived. The crest rail bears some resemblance to that used on an earlier chair, but is, in essence, a shaped bar of wood stuck onto two other shaped bars. Now this could be said of any chair, but almost all fine chairs of the previous century used classical architectural elements and ornaments in their structure. Early Victorian chairs began to seek new shapes – in this case the balloon. It was, of course, the time of the early balloonists, so no doubt the origin of the shape was fashionable and easily recognizable. These chairs have rather straight sides to the balloon – they are only slightly waisted, rather like a hairpin, which was another term that was used to describe one of the new styles of back. The only ornaments are the classical stylized inverted lotus decoration on the legs, and the lotus splat in the middle of the back.

Above: These are two from a set of eight mahogany dining chairs, circa 1840. They have good, solid structure, a slight roll-over on the crest rail, but again the arms of the 'carver' come too far forward. However, once the design became established, many chairs were made that way and sitters just learned to accommodate themselves. Sometimes you are lucky enough to find such a chair with arms that fit under your dining table.

ENGLISH CHAIRS
1800 – 1840 PART II

Above: One of the more obvious styles of the Regency period was the black-and-gilt chair based on Greek, Etruscan and Roman designs. The maker of the chairs illustrated is a little confused – the front legs are X-shaped, the rear legs are standard 18th-century European. As you can see, he had a slight problem joining the side seat rails, which have to twist in their length. Etruscan is the name given to the community who lived in what is now called Tuscany at the time when Ancient Rome was founded.

Right: These are more usual, even though the paint is rather shabby. The design on the back and around the seat rails is called 'Greek key'. They are made from painted beech, circa 1810.

Above: Here we have two from a set of eight mahogany chairs, circa 1815. These have a slight Greek influence with the ebonized flèche (arrow) on the uprights and the key ornament on the crest bar.

Above: The black decoration in this case is actually solid ebony that has been let in. These chairs are beechwood and not grained to simulate another timber, which is odd. Very rarely was beech left as show wood. It is an excellent timber for chair-making, but is usually gilded, grained or painted. These were made around 1815 and are attributed to Gillows. They were in the late Helena Hayward's Collection.

Right: Two from a set of eight mahogany dining chairs, circa 1815. The crossbar is carved with anthemion (honeysuckle) flower buds. These were a very popular classical Greek ornament. Note that in this set the carver arms are set back just a little.

Above: These are two from a set of ten chairs that sold recently for over £1,000 (US$1,800) each. I include them because of their shabby state. This cream-and-gilt decoration is original Regency paintwork, circa 1815. Do not dismiss furniture just because it looks old and shabby. If this set of chairs had been stripped and painted, as so often happens on television 'makeover' programmes, their value would have been greatly reduced.

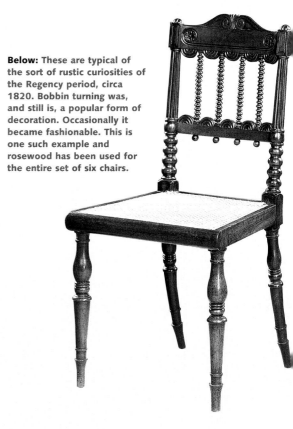

Below: These are typical of the sort of rustic curiosities of the Regency period, circa 1820. Bobbin turning was, and still is, a popular form of decoration. Occasionally it became fashionable. This is one such example and rosewood has been used for the entire set of six chairs.

Above: These are mahogany chairs, circa 1800, made to a design by Gillows. They are of the usual Gillows quality and show some of the range of designs produced by that great firm. You get the feeling that all the client needed to do was name a design – in this case 'trellis' – and a perfect trellis-back chair would be produced.

Below: These are standard brass-inlaid rosewood armchairs with double sabre legs, circa 1815. Good quality, comfortable chairs.

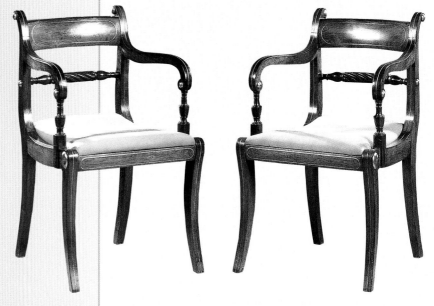

Below: These mahogany chairs were made in the provinces, circa 1815. The sign of provincial furniture is that the design incorporates some new element (in this case the rope-twist bar) together with older elements (the seat and leg construction is mid 18th-century).

Above: This rosewood chair is typically William IV. It has rather sudden curves and, although it still uses classical scrolls and other motifs, the back looks rather contorted. The cane seat is intended to have a loose squab cushion tied on with ribbons.

Left: These are very splendid chairs after a design by Morgan & Sanders, circa 1815. They are also known as Carlton House chairs, because such chairs are said to have been produced for Carlton House. An advertisement for similar chairs has been found. The text says that these chairs 'exhibit a judicious combination of elegance and usefulness...'. They are ebonized beech and parcel-gilt. They are also, almost needless to say, very prone to damage!

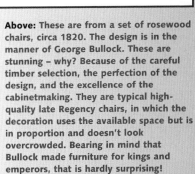

Above: These are from a set of rosewood chairs, circa 1820. The design is in the manner of George Bullock. These are stunning – why? Because of the careful timber selection, the perfection of the design, and the excellence of the cabinetmaking. They are typical high-quality late Regency chairs, in which the decoration uses the available space but is in proportion and doesn't look overcrowded. Bearing in mind that Bullock made furniture for kings and emperors, that is hardly surprising!

Right: This is a mahogany hall-chair, from the first quarter of the 19th century. Hall chairs were intended for occasional use, not for prolonged sitting, hence the solid seat. This example bears a painted crest and would, no doubt, have been made specifically for the family whose crest is shown.

UNUSUAL ENGLISH CHAIRS 1800 – 1840

Left: This style is known as a Glastonbury chair. The name is derived from the alleged use of this type of chair by the last abbot of Glastonbury (Somerset, England) at the time of the Dissolution of the Monasteries by Henry VIII. This example is in yew and was made in the second quarter of the 19th century.

Left and right: A mahogany metamorphic library-armchair, circa 1820, after a design by Morgan and Saunders. Morgan and Saunders held the patent for this design and were specialists in metamorphic furniture. In this version the back hinges backwards to provide the steps. These were mentioned in 'Regency Patent Furniture' by G. Bernard Hughes, Country Life, 2 January 1958, and in 'Morgan and Saunders and the Patent Furniture Makers of Catherine Street' by Brian Austen, Connoisseur, Vol. 187, No. 753, November 1974.

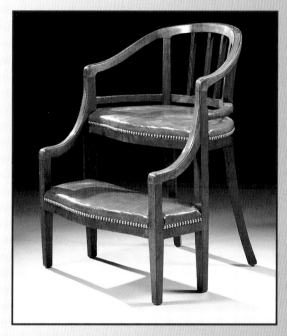

Above: This is a pair of bed steps, circa 1800. They are of chair form so they warrant inclusion here. Georgian beds were high, ponderous affairs and getting into them might have proved difficult for the elderly. Bed steps were also made to incorporate commodes, but these are rarely seen nowadays.

Above and below: This is another version of the metamorphic chair, in mahogany, circa 1825. The back of this chair hinges to fold forward, the crest rail rests on the ground and forms a support for the library steps that are revealed. These chairs look ugly but they are in fact very useful and desirable.

> " These chairs look ugly but they are in fact very useful and desirable "

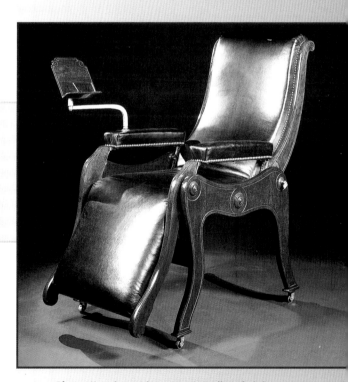

Above: Here is a curious patent reading-chair in mahogany. There is no indication of the maker, nor the date, but it was probably made in the second quarter of the 19th century. This would seem to be one of the less successful patent chairs.

Left: Now here is a different cup of tea! This all-singing, all-dancing library armchair with a sprung reclining back, circa 1835, bears the stamped mark T. Kilby. Sadly there is no written evidence for this maker. His work, however, speaks loudly of careful thought and planning. Although working in the William IV period, when furniture designs tended to be heavy, the maker has managed to build a solid, comprehensively equipped, elegant armchair.

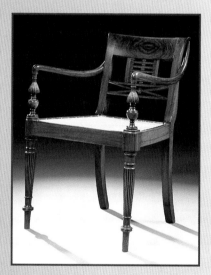

Left: This is from a set of ten Anglo-Indian rosewood armchairs, circa 1835. Overall they look European, but the timber sections are just a little heavy. A major clue, of course, is that the timber is Indian rosewood, not South American. The arms are suspended from the crest rail, which was an early 19th-century design. In this case the arms are said to be fashioned to resemble elephant tusks – but I am not entirely convinced.

Above: This is an Anglo-Indian library armchair, circa 1835. The timber is padauk. The general shape, the scrolled arms and the reeded legs are British in style while the scrolled leafwork in the panels of the rails and uprights is Indian. Indian furniture-makers proved themselves very good at copying European designs in native timbers. Where a design feature, such as a particular leaf motif, was familiar to them, they tended to use a native version of that design. However, the reeding and volute scrolls were new to the makers and these were closely copied in the European style, albeit somewhat stiffly.

Left: These strange objects are rustic chairs, made in the first half of the 19th century. The frames are made from natural branches that have had the bark removed. The branches were then painted, and the seats made out of rush. They look rickety but are in fact very sound. The stretchers are socketed into the legs in the normal way of Windsor chairs. The inner seat frames are jointed and glued to make strong structures to which the legs, backs and facings are fitted. They are not very comfortable but are most effective in giving the appearance of the rustic cottage furniture made fashionable by Wordsworth and Scott.

Below: These are simple oak chairs in the Gothic style popular in the early 19th century. They are sometimes known as 'Abbotsford' furniture, referring to the house lived in by Sir Walter Scott – not because they actually came from that house, but in recognition of the style of Gothic furniture popularized by the novelist. The legs are formed of cluster columns and the backs are shaped like lancet windows.

Above: Here is a pair of chairs made from bamboo in the first quarter of the 19th century. They are made to a Chinese pattern, using intricate joints and tiny wooden pegs, but were probably made in Britain – whether by Chinese or British workmen is not known. The fashion for Chinese furniture developed through the influence of the Prince of Wales, who had similar chairs supplied for the Royal Pavilion in Brighton, England.

Left: This is a simulated rosewood music stool with chair back, circa 1820. The lyre forming the back splat gives the stool a musical association and the top revolves on a large wooden screw, thus raising or lowering the seat.

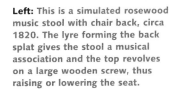

Above: A pair of mahogany hall chairs, circa 1810, attributed to Gillows. These have wonderful scallop-shell backs, all made and carved from the solid. The quality of these chairs is obvious in design, timber selection and execution.

Left: This must be a unique chair! It is a carved oak library chair, circa 1815. The provenance of the chair is Irish. The form is that of two massive griffins supporting a button-upholstered seat and back. The design is derived from the Hellenistic marble throne forming part of the Arundel Marbles at the Ashmolean Museum in Oxford, England.

ENGLISH UPHOLSTERED
CHAIRS 1800 – 1840

Left: This is rather a hangover from the previous century. It is known as a library chair. It can be used at a table or desk, but is more likely to be placed near a fire or a window, depending upon the season, in order that the reader can lean back, put their legs out and relax. The supports are very 18th-century, but button-upholstered leather is typical of the second quarter of the 19th century. It was probably made by a provincial chair-maker for a client who liked the old Georgian style but who appreciated the comfort of the 'modern' upholstery.

Right: A Regency mahogany tub chair – shaped like a barrel or tub – circa 1810. These chairs are wonderful for snuggling into. Once again, this is a type of library chair. The only way of dating this chair is by looking at the legs, bearing in mind that tub chairs returned to fashion in the early 19th century. Simple ring-turned legs, normally associated with the last years of the 18th century, stopped being used on this type of chair by about 1815.

Below: A pair of library bergères, circa 1820. A bergère is a chair with cane back and sides. The beech frames have a simulated rosewood finish, but most of this has worn off.

Above: A pair of gilt wood armchairs for use in a drawing room, circa 1815. These are rather French in style. The only stamp on the chairs is VR and a crown, indicating that they were formerly in the collection of Queen Victoria. Furniture made by émigré French craftsmen, working in London, was supplied to the Royal Palaces in the early 19th century. Chairs like this were made both as pairs and as long sets of 20 or more – and all the increments in between, depending on the customer's wishes.

Below: These are two more bergères illustrating the diversity of shapes produced. The tub-shaped chair is circa 1820; the model with scrolled arms and a high back dates from around 1835.

Below: A pair of carved gilt wood chairs, circa 1825, in the manner of Morel and Hughes. These chairs are derived from the 1815 model above, but with much greater decoration and opulence. That approach to furniture decoration was very characteristic of the George IV period, and to a greater and almost overbearing extent of the William IV period. Morel and Hughes were leading London cabinetmakers.

Below: A set of six mahogany library chairs, circa 1825. These are very elegant and comfortable. The front legs are carved with inverted lotus flowers. Note that castors are beginning to appear on chair legs. Castors were used on 18th-century chairs, but were usually very small and hidden in a recess up inside the foot.

Above: An elegant rosewood library or desk chair, made circa 1825. These legs and the general shape are more Regency than the next chair, which might be thought to be of similar age.

Above: An upholstered library armchair, circa 1825. I have included a number of such straightforward chairs in order to try to show the wide range of models made between 1800 and 1840.

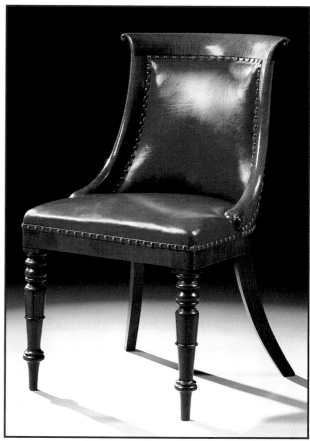

Above: A simple rosewood library or desk chair, made circa 1830.

Right: A mahogany library armchair, made circa 1835. The decoration on this chair has moved away from the Regency style and into cumbersome William IV which was the precursor to the Early Victorian style.

Above and Below: These are a pair of very typical early-Victorian carved mahogany library armchairs. They are covered in rather tired-looking brown hide. The white appearance of the polish is because the chairs have become damp, presumably while in storage, and a white bloom has formed on the polish. These are very mediocre chairs, made without much thought given to proportion or design. The seats look uncomfortable, but there is no height for a leather-covered squab cushion. I suspect the seats are a bit short on springs as well. Castors have now become big and ungainly.

Above: This is from a 16-piece suite supplied by George Morant in 1838. The style is French 'Louis XIV'. This term is used to describe furniture based upon 18th-century French rococo and 'Versailles' styles. The timber is walnut, parcel-gilt. The webbing under the seat bears the stencilled mark of the maker. The top covers have been removed but the original plaited gimp (braid) still remains.

ENGLISH UPHOLSTERED CHAIRS 1800 – 1840 153

ENGLISH SETTEES
1800 – 1840

Left: A painted chair-back settee in neo-classical style, circa 1800. These are very popular and elegant but often have restored decoration. Look closely under a good light. The frame is beech. The seat is caned and would normally be fitted with a long squab cushion.

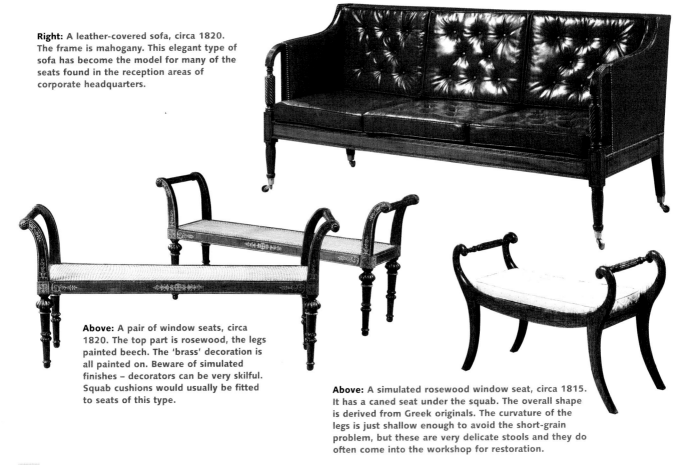

Right: A leather-covered sofa, circa 1820. The frame is mahogany. This elegant type of sofa has become the model for many of the seats found in the reception areas of corporate headquarters.

Above: A pair of window seats, circa 1820. The top part is rosewood, the legs painted beech. The 'brass' decoration is all painted on. Beware of simulated finishes – decorators can be very skilful. Squab cushions would usually be fitted to seats of this type.

Above: A simulated rosewood window seat, circa 1815. It has a caned seat under the squab. The overall shape is derived from Greek originals. The curvature of the legs is just shallow enough to avoid the short-grain problem, but these are very delicate stools and they do often come into the workshop for restoration.

Right: A pair of oak window seats, circa 1825. These were placed in front of a large window. As the benches had no back, they did not obstruct the window and they could be sat upon from either side. The design of these is derived from a Roman original, as illustrated in Tatham's book, Ornamental Architecture Drawn from the Originals in Rome, **1799.**

Left: A George IV mahogany settee, circa 1830. Although this attempts to be elegant, it is rather ungainly. The maker has tried hard and has used all the scrolls, curves and ornament in his design book, but hasn't grasped the principle that underlying shape and form give elegance, not ornament added on afterwards. The legs appear to be far too spindly to support the top.

Right: A William IV rosewood sofa, circa 1830 – very solid, substantial and comfortable-looking. There is still a trace of Greek urns on the arms and anthemion on the crest rail.

Right: A William IV mahogany scroll-end sofa, circa 1835. It has rather squatter and less graceful feet than the rosewood sofa shown at the bottom of page 155 but still retains a sense of elegance, proportion and comfort.

Left: A mahogany sofa with scrolls, showing the typical heaviness of the fully developed William IV style around 1835. The feet cock out unnecessarily and the seat is uncomfortably deep. Cabinetmakers have a rather vulgar expression for this colour of mahogany, referring to the yellowish tone, which is regarded as unattractive.

Right: A pair of carved oak window seats, dating from the mid-19th century. These are in Gothic style, but it is almost impossible to say when they were made because this type of oak furniture was made throughout the century. The covers are modern copies of 19th-century William Morris-style prints.

Below: This is an Anglo-Indian carved padauk chaise longue, from the second quarter of the 19th century. This chaise longue has a detachable side, the removal of which will convert the piece into a day bed. As a day bed I'm sure that it would have been much in demand in the hot climate of India in the early 19th century. Day beds first appeared in the 17th century when they were simply chairs with elongated caned seats. They rather dropped out of use in the 18th century and then returned in some numbers in the 19th century as chaises longues and ottomans.

Above: This is a late William IV mahogany settee. I say late William IV rather than Victorian, because the classical influence is still visible, with the central wreath, carved terminals and inverted flower-bud carved supports. The Victorians liked their settees deep and comfortable, and preferred not to see the straight lines of the main rails. They liked these elements to be curved and preferably covered with upholstery.

Above: A carved oak sofa, circa 1840. This is typical of the Gothic Revival furniture made for remodelled Victorian country houses. This sofa was made for Lowther Castle, Westmorland, England. This piece demonstrates beautifully the Victorian liking for deep upholstered seats.

Above: A mahogany sofa, circa 1835. This is a most impractical piece of furniture – anyone who knows anything about timber strength and grain direction would be afraid to sit on it in case the legs snapped off. Although very curvaceous, the carving is shallow and the whole appearance ungainly and fanciful.

ENGLISH FURNITURE
EARLY VICTORIAN

The Victorian period divides itself naturally into two halves. Queen Victoria married Prince Albert of Saxe-Coburg-Gotha in 1840. Prince Albert devoted himself to good works and noble ideas. He was president of the Society of Arts, and he masterminded the Great Exhibition at Crystal Palace, London in 1851 which was a showcase for anything made in Britain, including furniture. Sadly, Prince Albert wore himself into the ground and he died in 1861. Queen Victoria was devastated and the country went into mourning. At that point the second half of the Victorian period began. In this section we look at furniture made during the happy early years of this style-setting couple's marriage.

Above: This circular rosewood pedestal table, circa 1840, is almost William IV. What brings it into the early Victorian period is the plainness of the tricorn plinth base and the plain faceted baluster column. This table is 4ft 3in (1295mm) wide. Circular tables of this size are sometimes called loo tables – the card game of loo was very popular in Victorian times. In general the smaller circular tables are loo tables. Players needed to be able to reach the centre of a card table easily. The larger tables are for sitting around to eat.

Right: This walnut pedestal desk was made around 1845. This is a neat little desk only 5ft (1524mm) wide, and is quite clearly Victorian. The upstand around the top is a mid-19th-century feature often found on washstands and bedside tables. The plain plinth and turned wood handles to the drawers are also Victorian features. The flutes in the columns are flat-bottomed, more like channels than flutes, and the column is very narrow above the baluster, giving the baluster a wide top shoulder. Both these characteristics are mid 19th-century and are probably the result of greater use of machining in manufacture. A viable carving machine was developed by Thomas Jordan in 1845.

THE FIVE MAIN INFLUENCES TO VICTORIAN FURNITURE DESIGN:

CLASSICALLY BASED PIECES
These were a watered-down continuation of the Ancient Greek and Roman styles.

LOUIS XIV
In contemporary literature these were called Louis XIV but in actual fact the designs were those used in Louis XV's reign. This was rococo in essence, which allowed curvilinear and naturalistic designs.

ELIZABETHAN
This was a Victorian interpretation of Elizabethan.

NATURALISTIC
Easy shapes derived from natural subjects. Not to be confused with art nouveau which came later and was deliberately asymmetrical.

GOTHIC (IN VARIOUS GUISES)

Design was considered very important and The South Kensington Museum in London was set up in 1857 to display what was considered the best in ornamental art. This museum was renamed The Victoria and Albert Museum in 1899.

Above right: This is a rosewood 'what-not' (or set of shelves), circa 1840. The improvements in woodworking machinery meant that it was now possible to cut thinner veneers. Old 'double knife-cut' veneer – roughly 0.05in (1.2mm) thick – had been replaced by 'single knife-cut' veneer at 0.025in (0.6mm). The use of highly figured Rio rosewood is a continuation from the Regency period. The 'classical' design is simply a watered-down version of Regency and William IV styles. The architectural gable-top to the back is Regency in origin. However the feet are of French inspiration.

Right: In the same vein, this is a rosewood canterbury, circa 1840. Originally the term 'canterbury' referred to a small table with partitions to hold cutlery and plates, supposedly first ordered by an Archbishop of Canterbury. Subsequently the term came to be used for a small container with divisions for music, which later, with the demise of sheet music, became a container for magazines.

Above and below: This illustrates another strand of Victorian design. It is a marble-topped pietre dure rosewood centre table, made circa 1845. The base is a combination of Louis XIV and curvilinear naturalistic design. Fashion had changed and rococo design had become acceptable again. This return to rococo allowed the Victorian carvers to demonstrate their skills, as shown on the very curly base of this table. The black marble top is inlaid with pictures in stone (pietre dure); this work was carried out in Derbyshire, England as a native alternative to Italian pietre dure.

Above: This cheval mirror dates from the 1840s. The frame is mahogany and has quasi-Greek decoration. Cheval mirrors were French in origin and became an essential accessory for the Victorian bedroom.

Below: Another piece of bedroom furniture was this large wardrobe, 9ft (2.74m) wide and veneered in satin birch. The drawers are stamped 'GILLOWS LANCASTER'. This actual piece of furniture is recorded in the Gillows Sketch Book for 1849. The price charged was £31 2s 4d.

Left: This shows another Victorian staple – the hall stand. This example is made from mahogany, circa 1850. The construction is very simple, but substantial tenons were needed to support the arms which might have gentlemen's heavy, wet woollen overcoats hung from them. The lower portion is a stick stand but also an umbrella stand – the tin tray would catch the drips from soaked umbrellas.

Above: Another strand of Victorian design is shown in this rosewood-veneered octagonal library table in 'Elizabethan Gothic' style. The Tudor period, of which Elizabeth I was the last monarch, began in 1485 and ended in 1603. The Gothic period extended from about AD 1100 to AD 1400, so the Victorians were lumping together several centuries of furniture-making and calling it all by one name. In this table we have bun feet and spiral turning from 100 years later than Elizabeth I, along with tapered Gothic spires from 200 years before Elizabeth I. The whole Elizabethan style was based upon a romantic ideal of what English furniture in the 'Golden Age of Elizabeth' might have looked like. It was this kind of ignorance of historical accuracy that so annoyed later designers.

Above and Left: The last two photos show the base and top of a finely figured walnut centre table, circa 1850. The table closely resembles that shown in a book published in 1850, Designs for Furniture, by W. Smee & Sons. The top is 4ft 6in (1372mm) in diameter, which means that the book-matched leaves of figured walnut are 2ft 3in (686mm) wide. This is not exceptional, but it was a challenge to cut very thin veneer to fit such a size. Such pieces were designed to show off the way in which machining improvements permitted impressive visual statements.

CONTINENTAL CHAIRS
1800 – 1850 PART I

The first 50 years of the 19th century were full of political activity and new ideas. Furniture manufacture was equally eventful. At the beginning of the century the output of furniture-makers was small, their clientele was small in number, and the makers used designs based on originals drawn by the 'Great Designers' of the period. By 1820 manufacturing methods had changed, the clientele had enlarged enormously and the need for great designs had disappeared. Almost anything sold, and makers began to try out strange and fanciful designs.

Above: This splendid Directoire mahogany desk armchair, circa 1800, is attributed to Henri Jacob (1753–1824). The influences are still those of classical antiquity. This chair has more in common with the 18th century than the 19th.

Above: These chairs are Italian and were made about the same date as the previous item. Italian furniture was more forward-looking than that of other European countries. These chairs, with their swept arm supports, animal front legs and outward-scrolled rear legs, were ten years ahead of their northern-European counterparts.

Above: These chairs are also Italian, circa 1800. The neo-classical elements in the carved and gilded decoration closely resemble designs prepared for the Palazzo Reale in Milan in the last years of the 18th century. However, they are interpreted with 19th-century overtones in the form of the rectangular back panel, the tri-form rear legs and the rather stubby, ungraceful front legs.

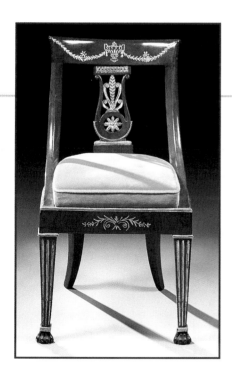

Above: An Italian chair, circa 1810. The mahogany show-wood is painted with leafy swags. The splat is lyre-shaped and centred with an anthemion.

This is a splendid detail of the side elevation of one of a pair of Italian gilt wood sofas, circa 1810. The elevation looks like an illustration taken from one of the classical drawing books. It may well have been made as part of the refurnishing of the Italian palaces.

Right: One from a set of eight French Restoration mahogany armchairs, circa 1820, attributed to Pierre-Gaston Brion. The design has now moved away from the bold curves of the 18th century. Classical motifs from the Empire period, such as the anthemion mount and the stars on the back panel, continue to be used, but the harsh, straight lines of Empire furniture have been relieved by slender, graceful curves. The rich mahogany is carved almost as if it were stone.

Below: This settee is French, circa 1812, and is attributed to Pierre-Gaston Brion (worked circa 1800–38). The decoration includes laurel, myrtle and ribbon-tied rushes. All of these have classical Roman significance. The front legs are in the form of plain columns.

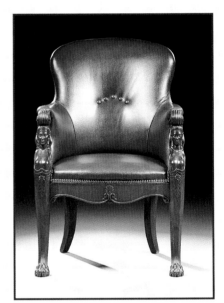

Above right: This is an Italian desk armchair, circa 1815, in mahogany. The Egyptian figures are based on classical originals but have become slightly softened in form, as have the legs and overall appearance. This 'softening' of detail is a sure sign of 19th-century origin.

Right: A French Restoration mahogany revolving armchair, circa 1820. Revolving chairs began to be made in the early 19th century. This model does have deeply scrolling arms, reminiscent of the previous century, but the mean, stubby, hock-type legs place it firmly in the 19th century.

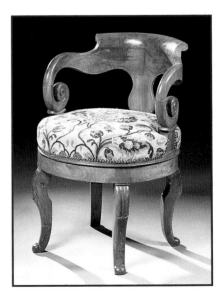

Below: A set of six parcel-gilt mahogany armchairs, circa 1820, attributed to Jacob Desmalter (1770–1841). This design is Empire in taste. The powerful hoof feet and the swan, which is a proud and imperious bird, all allude more to Empire than French Restoration style. The supports below the seat rail show how bold such a leg can be when designed by a master. Compare these to the 'hock' legs on the revolving chair opposite.

Above: A French Restoration mahogany armchair with deeply curved back, raised on lion monopodia. Removal of the upholstery shows the simple seat construction, which has changed little over the years.

Right: A mahogany armchair, Empire, circa 1820. This is an example of the overlapping of styles. Politically the Empire was dead by 1820, but the style continued to be used by some makers. Compared to the pair of rectangular-backed, carved and gilded Italian chairs on page 163, this chair retains the austere lines of the Empire style.

CONTINENTAL CHAIRS
1800 – 1850 PART II

Left: A carved mahogany desk armchair, circa 1825. This is in the Restoration style, exemplified by the bulbous legs, rolled-over top to the crest rail and general 'comfortableness' of the whole chair. By 1825 the concern for comfort rather than purity of style was becoming paramount.

Right: Two chairs from an Italian suite of chairs and sofa, made around 1825. These are very similar to some of the neo-classical Regency designs found in Britain. The British designs were based upon original classical ornamentation found in Italy and Greece, so the similarity is hardly surprising.

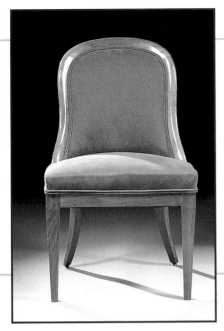

Above: Two from a set of ten mahogany armchairs, Restoration style, circa 1835. These are an example of the plain and simple furniture which began to be mass-produced around this date. The arms are the only feature that require special skills.

Above: One from a set of ten rosewood chairs in Biedermeier style, circa 1830. The Biedermeier style started in Germany and Austria in the third and fourth decades of the 19th century and then spread throughout Europe. The term Biedermeier was not coined until much later – Papa Biedermeier was a cartoon character whose opinions were always bland and middle-of-the-road. The bland furniture which became commonplace throughout Europe was named after this character. Biedermeier was based on the Empire style but was imitating the meubles de luxe. The middle classes for whom the furniture was made couldn't afford the labour-intensive work of the grand furniture of the Empire or the 18th century. The results are local interpretations, mixing sophisticated motifs with naive proportions and techniques. In essence Biedermeier is comfort on a lightly classical foundation.

Below: This is an Italian walnut and marquetry méridienne, circa 1830. A méridienne is a short sofa, almost a window seat. It is raised on reeded toupie feet. Toupie refers to the shape of a spinning top, the old-fashioned child's toy.

Above: One of a set of six painted fruitwood Biedermeier chairs, made around 1830. One of the characteristics that developed in the 19th century is the passion for using different timbers. This was more common in south Germany and Austria. It is hard to ascribe an origin to this chair; the crest rail is Regency, the legs date from the 1830s and the knees are rather William IV. Compared to the previous illustration there is little plain and bland about it, but the combination of styles, the fact that it is Continental in manufacture and the date of the latest ornamentation all point to the Biedermeier ethic rather than any other style.

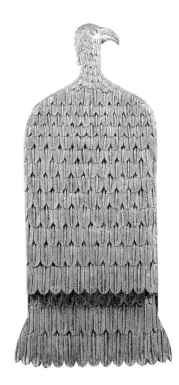

Above: A set of six mahogany, brass-mounted and ebony-inlaid early 19th-century Baltic dining chairs. The Empire style lingered on in north-eastern Europe. These chairs have a classical austerity which was evidently appreciated in the Baltic countries. The spherical turnings at the top of the front legs have a broad flat band edged with gilt brass mouldings. Similar mouldings are shown on the inside edges of the recessed back panels. Thinly applied brass mouldings are frequently found on 19th-century Baltic and Russian furniture. Such mouldings are very difficult to repair, as they are of unique section.

Above: This splendid carved chair is Russian and dates from the first half of the 19th century. The chair has traces of gilding throughout. It seems to be an example of early 19th-century Romantic-style historicism. There was a movement in the early part of the 19th century which derived its inspiration from medieval art. Such instances of turning to much earlier periods for inspiration are not confined to Russia – they occur in France, Germany and Britain – but this is one of the most striking examples I have seen.

Left: A Russian Karelian birch and carved gilt wood day bed, made circa 1840. The use of pale-coloured decorative timbers (bois clairs) seems to have originated in France and then spread eastward through Europe. Austria and Russia became the main exponents. Karelian birch (Betula pendula **Roth**) – a form of spalted birch – was especially popular with Russian makers.

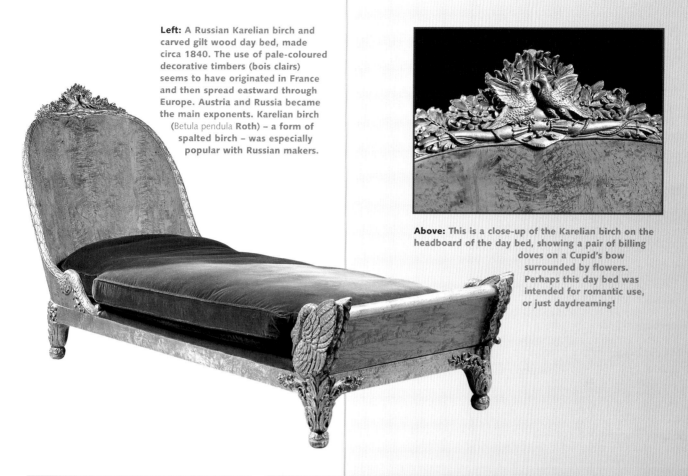

Above: This is a close-up of the Karelian birch on the headboard of the day bed, showing a pair of billing doves on a Cupid's bow surrounded by flowers. Perhaps this day bed was intended for romantic use, or just daydreaming!

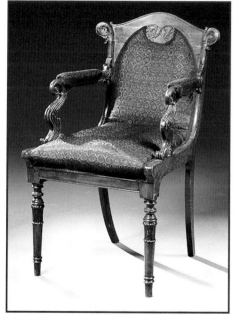

Above: Moving further across Europe, this mahogany armchair is Danish in the manner of the architect Hetsch (1788–1864). There is not room to study it here, but Danish furniture of the 19th century is quite distinctive. The legs, both front and rear, are standard 19th-century; but the arms and back decoration are noticeable for the increased use of carving. Scandinavian carving is legendary, and I suspect there was a nationalistic element in the designs for this chair.

Above: Two from a set of 18 mahogany chairs, Restoration in style, circa 1850. The dark, heavily figured timber is indicative of Dutch construction. The use of glue blocks indicates mid 19th-century origin, as do the narrow section of the front legs and the deep crest rail. The overall artistic inspiration is French Restoration – the style of another country 25 years earlier. This intermingling of styles and dates typifies the problems of dating 19th-century furniture.

CONTINENTAL FURNITURE 1830 – 1850

As Europe headed towards the middle years of the 19th century, ordinary furniture went into the doldrums. Certainly there were commercial exhibitions, for which items of outstanding design or construction were made. However, the main output of makers was factory-produced, of indifferent quality and unremarkable design. For the purposes of this study, the remainder of the 19th century is divided into three eras: that made between 1830 and 1850, which was fairly quiet on the domestic furniture front; that made between 1850 and 1880, which was becoming more enlivened; and that made from 1880 to 1900, which was far from quiet!

Left: This is a French mahogany bibliothèque (bookcase) dating from the 1830s. Although the mounts are Empire style, the thinness of the machine-cut veneers, the squatness of the cornice and the plainness of the flat surfaces belong to a later era. Though the grandeur of The Empire had ended 20 years earlier, the styles lingered on in a watered-down way.

Right: Furniture that was made in Italy is more interesting. This shows a pair of columnar side tables, made circa 1835 in cherry. This maker has taken the base of a column, raised it on feet and given it a cupboard and a drawer. A marble top completes the effect. They are 2ft 6in (762mm) high and 1ft 8in (508mm) wide.

Above: Another example of furniture based on Pelagio Palagi's designs is shown here. This is a fruitwood and amaranth console table, circa 1835. The top of this table, although composite, is still very much a 'slab top'. Classical Roman furniture was perceived as made from slabs of marble, and this piece is in that vein. It has a big, heavy top raised on scrolled classical supports. However, it is clearly 19th-century, not earlier, because of the abundance of flat surfaces, particularly in the plinth and frieze, and also the stiffness and mathematical precision of the scrolls and their decoration.

Above: This shows an Italian walnut centre table, inlaid with ivory, mother-of-pearl and ebony, on a carved and gilded base. The table, which is 3ft (914mm) in diameter, dates from about 1840. It shows the combination of naturalistic sculpture in the base – rockwork, vines, flowers and animals – with the finely inlaid marquetry top.

Above: We return to more formal Italian furniture with the card table shown here. It is based on designs by Pelagio Palagi and was probably made around 1840. The body is rosewood and the pale-coloured marquetry is maple. Palagi's designs ranged from the Etruscan, shown here, to the neo-Gothic.

Above: At first glance this next piece might appear similar. In fact this is a birchwood cabinet, probably Russian, made in the mid 1830s. Although there is a lot of inlaid decoration, it is a very plain cabinet. The mirrored interior is of architectonic form, but the repetitive bands of zigzag and curled decoration are not very inspiring. The veneers are thin, the carcass is crudely made and the whole piece is graceless.

Above: Although it looks rather like the entrance to a Metro tunnel, this bookcase is a much finer piece of furniture than the last piece. It is of Austrian or German origin, 7ft 8in (2.34m) wide and veneered in mahogany. This is a simple piece, showing that all you need to make attractive furniture is good materials and good proportions.

Above: A good mahogany secrétaire desk is shown here. This is probably Belgian, circa 1830. The front legs are formed of winged lion monopodia.

Below: A pair of neo-classical ebonized wood and parcel-gilt jardinières, made in about 1845. Such plant holders might have been made in Northern Europe or in Italy; they were very popular.

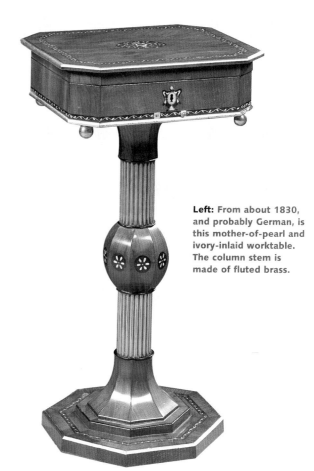

Left: From about 1830, and probably German, is this mother-of-pearl and ivory-inlaid worktable. The column stem is made of fluted brass.

Below: This is a maple and amaranth worktable, made in about 1835 in Charles X fashion. Charles X only ruled France for six years, but the style of furniture associated with him lasted a little longer. It is characterized by symmetry and neat lines, as shown in this little table.

Above: A fine and unusual pair of German Biedermeier mahogany tables is shown here. These are not run-of-the-mill Biedermeier. The bases are formed from dolphin supports with swan-head tails resting on a plinth, which is raised upon the backs of a pair of turtles. The gilt metal wreaths around the friezes are later additions. All in all, it is a pretty fantastic concoction, designed to please the nouveaux riches.

Below: Here is an unusual Biedermeier fruitwood writing desk, made in Vienna, circa 1830. Curved components were rather a trademark of the Biedermeier style. The piece is attributed to Joseph Danhauser (1720–1829) who owned the most important furniture factory in Vienna in the early 19th century. A collection of some 2,500 designs from his factory is now in the Österreichisches Museum für Angewandte Kunst in Vienna. If you are visiting the region, don't forget the Thonet Museum in Frankenberg.

CHAPTER

FIVE

The Victorian Era
and Artistic Revival

ENGLISH FURNITURE
MID-VICTORIAN

The middle years of the Victorian period were a time of mourning for Queen Victoria and her court, a time of consolidation for the makers of conventional furniture, experimentation for the entrepreneurs and new thinking for the idealists.

Left: This is a walnut and marquetry centre table, circa 1860. Designed in Continental style, it looks neither English nor really Louis XIV. The burr-walnut and marquetry top is normal English of the period, but the thick concave fins of the column splaying out into a wide tri-form base is rather Germanic in origin.

Right: This is a lady's papier-mâché desk with stationery compartment, writing slope and needlework compartment, circa 1850. Although it isn't a wooden object, it would be unfair not to mention the use of papier-mâché in the 19th century. The firm of Jennens and Bettridge was the best-known manufacturer. They perfected a treatment that produced highly durable articles. Trays, chairs, small settees and even beds were made in papier-mâché. The surfaces were usually finished in black lacquer and decorated with gilding, painted scenes and mother-of-pearl. The Victorians were very innovative and tried all sorts of materials for making furniture – cast iron and brass are well known. Ebony-type ornaments were made from a mixture of dark sawdust and animal blood. Carton-pierre was made from paper pulp, whiting and glue; being lighter in weight than traditional compo it was therefore used for large expanses of decoration. Both bentwood and plywood were used in the 19th century.

> " *Robinson became widely known and carved several other pieces, but the Chevy Chase sideboard remains his best-known work and is considered to be the most famous piece of Victorian carved furniture.* "

Left and below: The Chevy Chase sideboard was carved between 1857 and 1863 by Gerrard Robinson (1834–91) of Newcastle, England. The name is derived from the 15th-century ballad of Chevy Chase, a popular song about the rivalry between two great northern families – the Percys and the Douglases. Robinson attended the Newcastle School of Design and served an apprenticeship as a carver and gilder. Large sideboards of this type were popular at the Great Exhibition in 1851, and the firm for which Robinson then worked produced several. He subsequently set up his own firm, which produced the Chevy Chase sideboard. Robinson became widely known and carved several other pieces, but the Chevy Chase sideboard remains his best-known work and is considered to be the most famous piece of Victorian carved furniture. The oak sideboard is 11ft (3.35m) wide and 9ft (2.74m) high. The panels are carved in high relief. The overall style is hard to define – it is High Victorian with naturalistic carving in a Jacobean-inspired cabinet.

Above and right: Two more satin-birch pieces are shown here. The writing table bears a paper label inscribed 'H.H. Prince Leopold Room'. Prince Leopold was the fourth son of Queen Victoria. The writing table and the side cabinet were sold at an auction in Cowes on the Isle of Wight, England. It is possible, therefore, that they formed part of the furnishings of Queen Victoria's residence on the island, Osborne House. The side cabinet, sometimes called a chiffonier, is of typical form. The top and shelves would have been filled with ornaments. Both pieces were made around 1860.

Right: The oak washstand, which dates from about 1860, is a precursor to what became known as 'Victorian Progressive' design. It has simple lines and is inspired by medieval constructional methods. There is no attempt to hide the joints, and this 'revealed construction' became a trademark of the reformers – it's a method that is still influential today. The bearers of the underframe intersect like architectural beams. The curved braces are reminiscent of those found in roof timbers. Above all, it has a minimum of decoration. It was in fact an objection to the over-fussy furniture that was being produced at the same date.

Right: Here is another piece that eschews decoration. This is a satin-birch pedestal desk, dating from circa 1860. It is a straightforward functional piece relying for its only decoration on the rippled-satin appearance of the veneer. The drawers have simple turned knobs. When trying to date furniture by the handles or knobs, be aware that new handles were put on many pieces to comply with fashion. Look for signs of old, plugged pommel holes.

Right: A.W. Pugin (1812–52) began the work that resulted in Victorian Progressive design. The 'Reformers', as they became known, reacted against the mainstream of Victorian design. Their work, inspired by Ruskin, through William Morris and others, produced the stream of design that became the Arts and Crafts Movement. This then turned into the main 20th-century furniture design movement founded by such well-known figures as Gimson and the Barnsleys. The work of the 'Reformers' made acceptable the notion of a philosophic approach to making furniture. It is to these men that we owe a debt of thanks for the 'thinking' makers who appeared in the 20th century. Good early examples of Reformers' Gothic furniture are hard to find outside museums and private collections. This is a vernacular example – an octagonal walnut centre table raised on leaf-carved pillars. The piece is not over-decorated, nor does it have imagined Gothic decoration. The cruciform bearers have honest and simple trefoil carvings as stretchers.

Right: Now we go to the opposite extreme. This well-decorated walnut, marquetry and gilt-brass-mounted centre table was made in about 1860. The whole piece is in the French style. However, there are several notable differences between furniture made in the two countries. The English cabinetwork and structure are stronger. Note how far out the legs have to come to support the 4ft 9in (1448mm) diameter table, and also how thick and strong those legs, which end in massive carved claws, are. The gilt mounts are also English-made, and although you cannot see it in this photograph, the modelling on English mounts is normally far less crisp and detailed than that on a French ormolu.

ENGLISH FURNITURE
LATE VICTORIAN

Furniture in the late Victorian period falls into two categories. One is rich, fat, showy, big and comfortable, the other is new and honest. The establishment tended to prefer the former, while the latter consists of the Arts and Crafts Movement, art nouveau and the various off-shoots from those styles.

Above: First we have a typically Victorian serving table, in mahogany, circa 1860. The carving is bold, crisp, symmetrical and well proportioned. This piece exudes confidence and authority. The motto depicted on the ribbon is 'Post tenebras lux' (After darkness light), which was the motto of the Protestants during the Reformation. The bird on the top is a phoenix rising from the flames. Although the scroll brackets at each end of the back have a classical look about them, they are examples of 19th-century architectural carving. Look at any 19th-century bank or similar prestigious civic building in the high street and you will see scrolls like these. A nickname for this style is 'scroll and bracket'. In fact, looking up when walking around towns is a technique worth remembering. Modernization of shop fronts usually only takes place at ground-floor level, so you can see the original decoration left untouched on the first floor and above. Look upwards for the original carving and inspiration, but watch out for lamp posts!

Above: Here is a suitable bookcase for a prestigious building. This burr-walnut library bookcase was made around 1860. It is another piece that has a restrained elegance and a sense of power. Those who commissioned this and similar furniture were so rich that they didn't need to display their wealth ostentatiously. A simple Greek-key border alluding to the classical age of empires is sufficient to impress visitors.

Above: Just to bring us back to earth, here is an ordinary mahogany dining table, made about 1860. This is the sort of table that would have been stacked with food at Christmas in the dining room of a professional gentleman's Victorian town house. The legs, sometimes called 'billiard-table legs' due to their heaviness, are machine-turned and carved.

Below: This octagonal satinwood occasional table with a painted top was made around 1870. The painted decoration harks back to its use 100 years earlier when the Adam Brothers used Etruscan and Pompeian discoveries as inspiration. This table has an Italianate look, with its incurved legs.

Left: One name that has appeared with great frequency so far is that of Gillows. The firm was still in existence in 1868, and indeed furniture bearing their name is still sold today. This pair of oak open bookcases was made by Gillows around 1868 and the firm's records show that they cost £32 9s 4d. (£32.45, or US$58) The tops are flanked by fleur-de-lis (heraldic lily) finials carved with oak leaves and vines (see detail). The leather pelmets hanging below the shelves are to stop dust from settling on the top edges of the books. Note the use of linenfold panels in the end uprights. In this instance the Gothic ornamentation has not been overdone.

Right: This butler's tray on stand was made around 1870. In the late 19th century almost every activity had its own particular apparatus. Stands were made for trays, luggage, reading, smoking, newspapers, hanging clothes and towels, shaving, and holding cakes (known as the 'Curate's Joy'). Late 19th-century printed catalogues show a multitude of specialist articles that a furniture manufacturer could produce.

Left: Exhibitions of manufactured goods were a regular feature of the Victorian period. Some of the most notable were in 1851, 1855, 1862, 1867 and 1878. Makers vied with each other to produce stunning pieces – as they do now. Here is a satinwood side cabinet, of exhibition quality, circa 1870, with marquetry in ivory and ebony. The general style is classical. In the preceding 70 years the classical style had not been superseded, as had happened to the various styles in the middle of the 18th century – it had just been adapted and re-used again and again. Compared to 18th-century ideas of good taste this piece is over-decorated, although people would have approved of the actual subject matter of the decoration. By our standards today the decoration may look old-fashioned, but think how proud a marquetry specialist would be today to produce such a piece, even with the benefit of laser cutting techniques. Each age has its own style, and you would be a brave person to say that one style is 'better' than another. I happen to prefer an 18th-century treatment of this type of decoration, but I have to take my hat off to the sheer craftsmanship shown in this 1870 version.

Right: This rosewood boulle and gilt-bronze side cabinet was made around 1880. Sometimes these were called credenzas. The thin brass inlay is prone to lifting. If re-glued straight away there is little problem, but if the lifting decoration is not repaired it can become bent and distorted. Once damaged, the brass is very hard to re-lay. This one has a fair amount of tortoiseshell showing, but frequently they are black and sombre in overall appearance. The black and badly damaged examples were not popular in the antique market.

Right: This bedroom cabinet in satinwood, circa 1880, is in the manner of Holland and Sons. Such cabinets were less imposing than wardrobes but still contained tray shelves, drawers and a cupboard. They would be placed in dressing rooms and smaller guest bedrooms. Holland and Sons were one of the big names in late Victorian furnishing. The design is basically classical and is leading us towards the Edwardian revival of late 18th-century designs.

HISTORICAL DATES

1854	Outbreak of Crimean War
1855	Florence Nightingale reforms nursing
1859	Charles Darwin's **Origin of Species** published
1861	Abraham Lincoln becomes President of United States of America
1863	Lincoln proclaims the abolition of slavery in USA
1869	William Gladstone becomes Prime Minister of Great Britain
1871	Trade Unions legalized in Great Britain
1876	Battle of Little Big Horn Alexander Graham Bell invents the telephone
1877	Queen Victoria proclaimed Empress of India
1880	Boer revolt against the British in South Africa
1886	Gottlieb Daimler invents the internal combustion engine
1887	Golden Jubilee of Queen Victoria's reign
1895	Rhodesia founded by Cecil Rhodes; Wilhelm Roentgen discovers X-rays
1901	Death of Queen Victoria; accession of Edward VII
1910	Death of Edward VII; accession of George V
1914	Start of World War I

Above: Finally, here is a pair of satinwood and marquetry display cabinets from about 1900. These are in what is known as 'Sheraton Revival style'. The first decade of the 20th century produced well-made examples of classical English cabinetwork. The proportions, design, timbers and techniques are not quite right to be convincing 18th-century pieces – for example, the backboards may well be made of ply rather than solid wood, and the veneers are too thin – but this was the last period when large quantities of furniture using traditional styles and methods were made. Everything changed after The Great War.

ENGLISH AESTHETIC MOVEMENT

The period in the late 19th century known as English Aesthetic had its origins in the 'Reformers' movement, which started with A.W. Pugin. The Aesthetic Movement disliked the classical designs of the 18th century and looked for their inspiration to an interpretation of medieval English work, see pages 24–27.

Left: My first photograph shows a carved oak overmantel mirror, circa 1865. The crenellated top arches forward in medieval style. The arched canopy was a feature of furniture in pre-Tudor England. The use of embossed gilt leather, as seen in the overarching panels here, is another throwback to natural materials and handcraft techniques – although I doubt that many of the English Yeomanry had gilded leather panels in their houses. The overmantel was originally conceived as a mirror in a decorative surround to be placed over the mantelpiece. However, they were used in entrance halls and corridors as shelves, which had the added benefit of a mirror back.

Right: This is a satinwood writing table, circa 1870, attributed to Gillows. Apart from the fact that a similar table is recorded in the Gillows Estimate Sketchbooks, numbered 10753, the handles and the use of screws to hold the drawer linings are typical of Gillows. The style is faintly medieval with trestle-type splayed legs, but retains the fluting and reeding of classical furniture. The result, as one would expect from Gillows, is a very elegant table.

Left: Here we have an ebonized hanging cabinet, dating from about 1870, in the manner of E.W. Godwin. Godwin was an exponent of the 'Japanese' style. Now this cabinet may not look very Japanese, but the use of black ebonizing polish to produce an appearance similar to that of black lacquer was symptomatic of the interest in all things Japanese. The centre roundels on the doors are in the form of stylized chrysanthemums – a very important design element in Japanese art. The decoration is incised and gilded, and the cabinet measures 24in (610mm) in width.

Below: The maker of this unusual chair is unknown, but he certainly experimented with design. It dates from about 1875. The designer uses the extended front leg at a rakish angle to support the back. This is a topsy-turvy idea as far as chairs are concerned, although the maker was probably familiar with metamorphic library chairs. The padded back is reminiscent of a prie-dieu chair. The curls, flutes and zigzags are all typical of the aesthetic designers' struggle to find a new and satisfying form of decoration. In fact, no such new decorative ethos emerged until art deco. Art nouveau was based on other, albeit naturalistic, designs.

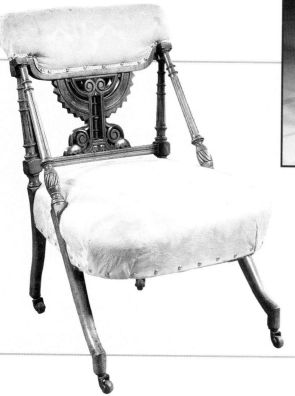

Above: Two ebonized chairs from about the same date are shown next. These are not radical in design. The smaller chair is based rather loosely on a Napoleon III design, and the other on a 'Glastonbury' chair (see page 146). Again, they have incised and gilded decoration. The larger chair has thuya-burr panels let into the uprights, in the manner of the Lamb firm of Manchester, England. The designer of these chairs could not really be called a Reformer, as the shapes are little changed from earlier designs, and the only concession to the ideology is the ebonizing to give them a faintly Oriental look. Lamb's was a prestigious firm, but they remained firmly at the conservative end of the market, eschewing really radical design.

ENGLISH AESTHETIC MOVEMENT 185

Left: A much more familiar item of Aesthetic furniture is shown here. This is a walnut side cabinet in the manner of Bruce James Talbert by Gillow & Co., circa 1875. Talbert provided an alternative to the High Victorian Gothic with his designs that were more accessible to the middle-class late-Victorian householder. Although this example is stamped 'Gillow & Co.', and was therefore at a premium, this style was seen again and again among vernacular house contents. Though used as a sideboard, the intention was for it to be an item of display furniture in the drawing room, not the dining room.

Below: This mildly Anglo-Japanese piece is an ebonized, painted satin-birch side cabinet, circa 1880. The basic form derives from an Elizabethan sideboard – shelves above, central drawers, cupboards and open spaces below. The painted panels are used in the same way that pietra-dura panels were used in the 17th century. The gallery is also a mid-17th-century touch. So really, the only new design features are the straight line, incised and gilded decoration, and the ebonizing in the Japanese style. Of course, ebonizing had been used 180 years earlier in a previous age of European fascination with the Orient. Straight lines have always been used as inlay, so perhaps this is an example of how even when Reformers try to come up with new and different designs, all they end up doing is repeating the past.

Below: We now move to something much more radical, almost presaging art nouveau. A macassar ebony and ebonized centre table, circa 1875, is shown here. The use of macassar ebony is unusual, but this timber became very popular in the art nouveau and art deco years. The elongated brass-cap castors are similar to mounts found on Japanese furniture and other articles. The gentle, organic splay of the legs is quite different to the medieval-based legs on other aesthetic centre tables. This has the air of the great Victorian designer E.W. Godwin.

Above and right: Before we leave the Reformers, I would like to mention Castell Coch, near Cardiff, Wales. This remarkable building was furnished by William Burges, circa 1875, and is well worth a visit. The cabinet and bed-frame shown in these photographs are pure fantasy, medieval Gothic. Although Burges and the other Reformers had intended to get away from the mass-produced, classically derived furniture, they often ended up creating extremely heavy designs, both visually and literally. It was hardly surprising, then, that there was an opposite stream of new design that took the name of art nouveau.

EVENTS WITHIN THE REFORMERS' MOVEMENT
PROGRESSIVE DESIGN – REFORMERS IN THE EARLY PERIOD:

1835 A.W. Pugin, 1812–52, son of Augustus Charles Pugin who also published a book, *Gothic Furniture*, based upon late medieval originals. A.W. Pugin was the designer in charge of the interior of the Palace of Westminster in London – now the Houses of Parliament.

A.W. Pugin hated 'sham' – he liked revealed construction. Detail should have a meaning and serve a purpose.

Simple furniture, the design of which originated with A.W. Pugin, was produced over a long period, about 1840–70.

1853 Ruskin's *Stones of Venice* published. The chapter on 'The Nature of Gothic' became an 'almost irresistible force' among designers in the 1860s.

1857 Gothic Revival painted cabinets began to be produced. These are an important innovation in Gothic Revival Furniture. They can be rather overbearing.

HIGH VICTORIAN PROGRESSIVE DESIGN:

1861 William Morris's firm founded. Webb, Seddon, Burges, Shaw and other makers worked for Morris. Their furniture began to be shown publicly after 1862. It was no longer Tudor Gothic that they turned to for inspiration, but the sterner 13th-century Gothic.

J.P. Seddon introduced diagonal panelling, which was adopted later by Bruce Talbert, Richard Charles and C.L. Eastlake.

1862 The Reformers' Gothic furniture at the London International Exhibition 'encouraged inflated ideas and overstatements of style among those who did not fully understand the philosophy and history behind the movement'. In the last years of the century, Charles Voysey was to deplore the influence of the big exhibitions.

1882 The founding of the Century Guild marked the formal beginning of the Arts and Crafts Movement.

WILLIAM MORRIS AND COMPANY

'William Morris revolutionised the public taste in domestic art' – from Morris's obituary in *The Art Journal*, 1896.

Morris's philosophy was based on that of Ruskin: 'What business have we with Art at all unless all can share it?'

Furniture associated with Morris was soundly constructed in conscious revolt 'against the shoddy, everyday products of commerce'. This itself was a mark of reform in the 1860s, but striking originality was not the distinguishing feature.

Some of Morris & Company's best cheap furniture was derived from simple specimens that had been found in the provinces.

In 1860 Ford Maddox Brown introduced a surface finish of green stain, which was applied to cheap bedroom furniture. This trademark green stain is often applied in an attempt to fool the observer into thinking that an item was made by Morris & Co.

CONTINENTAL
FURNITURE 1850 – 1880

I'm going to start this section on Continental furniture with some English furniture. This is because, in the middle of the 19th century, one of the strands of British furniture design was the 'Continental Style'. The first two photographs are of English pieces that look as though they were made on the Continent.

Left: A small rosewood-veneered bureau plat, mounted with Continental porcelain plaques, circa 1855. The plaques are painted with figures and flowers, with the exception of the end roundels, which carry the French royal monogram. This might be thought to indicate both a royal and a French connection, but from the mid 19th century the authority of the French royal family had waned and the monogram was used merely as a decorative device. The porcelain and gilt metal mounts would have been purchased in Paris, then incorporated in a French-style writing desk made by English cabinetmakers. To the uninitiated the piece looks French, but when you turn it up (as you should do with any piece of furniture before reaching a conclusion about its origins) the carcass will be oak, the dovetails finer and the general cabinetwork better quality than most French pieces of the time.

Right: The next table is another example of the same trail of events. This satinwood veneered table is 6ft (1830mm) in diameter and looks Continental by default. The base certainly doesn't look English, but don't be fooled; always examine the cabinetwork before deciding the country of origin – this is an English table successfully trying to look Continental.

Left: This shows a Napoleon III boulle and gilt-bronze bonheur-du-jour, circa 1860. Glazed doors replace the more usual stationery compartments and drawers above the folding writing surface. This piece is part display cabinet and part bureau. The cupboard would have held objects of virtu, or other precious items.

Above: Now we move on to real Continental furniture. Here is an ebony, ivory and gilt-bronze cabinet on a stand, circa 1860. It is in Renaissance style, the upper part formed as an oval cabinet, set with coloured hard stones, the stop-fluted columns supported by male terms. The open lower stand is formed of faceted baluster legs, similar to those used in the 17th century. Similar cabinets can be found in the Musée d'Orsay and the Musée des Arts Décoratifs, in Paris.

Right: Retrospective design is shown here. This is a Napoleon III ebonized wood and gilt-bronze side cabinet 39in (990mm) wide, made circa 1860. It has a marble top with glazed door below, enclosing shelves (now missing). The tapering spiral-fluted columns are raised on toupie feet. A down-pointed tapering spiral was a distinguishing decorative feature first used by André-Charles Boulle in the early 18th century.

Above: Here is another piece typical of those made in the third quarter of the 19th century. This is a thuja and ebony bureau de dame, signed 'DIEHL PARIS'. The display shelves are similar to those of an étagère, but rather meanly held up by tiny brass columns. The thuja is decorative but discreet, the trophy mounts polite and restrained. The whole piece speaks of repression and conformity – it's almost boring. The reaction to this ethos was the 'Naughty Nineties'.

Left: This French gilt brass and boulle console table was made circa 1860. It is a fairly standard design for the period, using ebony, brass and tortoiseshell, gilded metal, marble and porcelain. In a sense there is little else that you could put on this table! The move towards simpler designs that occurred at the end of the century was in reaction to this sort of piece. The maker felt obliged to fill every available space with decoration, and the buying public loved it.

Right: Another over-decorated piece is this little guéridon table, made circa 1860. A guéridon was originally a tall candle-stand with a tripod base, but gradually the stand became lower until it became the size of a normal small circular table.

Below: A better understanding of design and proportion is shown by the maker of this amboyna, ebonised wood and porcelain secrétaire. Large wall cabinets containing cupboards, mirrors, drawers and shelves were being made on both sides of the Channel between the mid-19th century and the start of The Great War. Without the aid of the maker's marks on details like locks, it is often hard to decide which country they were made in. As I have said before, generally the cabinetwork was better in England and generally the gilt metalwork was better in France. The French used the term bronzier to describe a maker of bronzes, and generally speaking they had a much better quality output for furniture mounts than the English did.

Above: The response to the mediocre designs of the 1870s is shown here. This is a wonderful side cabinet, made circa 1880 after an original by André-Charles Boulle. The workmanship and techniques used are described on pages 40–3; but in this example you can see the spiral fluting on the toupie feet properly executed.

Right: This little jardinière with bent legs is an example of the excesses of French design around 1870. The legs undulate between cabriole and serpentine, reflecting the paucity of design that led both to a revival of classic 18th-century designs and to the new art nouveau in France.

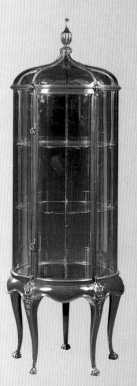

Right: A circular centre vitrine in mahogany. Although this has ball and claw feet and an urn finial, which are both 18th-century features, the concept of a 'see-through' piece of furniture with swept curves in the glazing bars and frieze is a harbinger of art nouveau.

CONTINENTAL
FURNITURE 1880 – 1910

The last years of the 19th century were known as 'La Belle Epoque', The Beautiful Period. This period was a time of great excitement for the arts. Sometimes furniture is accorded a minor place in the history of a period's 'artistic pursuits', but for the last years of the 19th century, French furniture and sculpture once more led the world.

Above: You may be forgiven for thinking that I have relapsed 120 years in my choice of the bureau plat shown here. It does look very similar to the Louis XV example on page 59. Even the timber is the same – kingwood. In the later piece the mounts are fuller and more flamboyant and the curves of the leg and frieze are deeper and more exaggerated. Stylistically, therefore, this example looks later, and this can be deduced from a distance. If one turned the piece upside down, the construction would give it away. The veneer is much thinner on the modern piece, there is less wear on the drawers, the carcass timbers are square all round, without saw marks and rough edges, and the general benchwork is better than it need be.

Left: Another example of a 'perfect' piece of furniture. This is a side cabinet with a central clock, again in kingwood, circa 1880. The marquetry and the cabinetwork are very precise. The design inspiration is 18th-century but there is a certain 'lightness' about the piece that identifies it as 19th-century.

Above and left: These two circular cabinets have similar design origins and date from the 1890s. Their mounts are much plainer, and the cabinetwork is straightforward and unsophisticated.

Above: Another piece of furniture that would be recognized by an 18th-century gentleman. This is another side cabinet, this time with 'plum-pudding' veneer, circa 1880. The decoration is more restrained, verging towards the Transitional, see pages 62–5.

Below: A bijouterie table, circa 1890. Again it has simple mounts and straightforward cabinetwork. Glass-topped tables were very popular towards the end of the century, as were display cabinets. Glass could now be made much thicker and with fewer blemishes to cause distortion of the objects inside. The display surface is velvet-lined.

Above: Many thousands of bonheur-du-jours (see pages 86–9) were made in the late 19th century, both in France and in Britain. This good example from France, circa 1890, is kingwood and gilt-brass, with a porcelain plaque set in the door. A nice touch, indicating that this is a better example, is the use of ebony on the inside chamfers of the serpentine legs. The flat surface folds forward to reveal a leather-inset writing surface. This piece is in need of repair: there are chipped veneers and the sabot (foot mount) is missing from the front left leg.

Right: Another Louis XV-style piece is shown here. This is a carved marble-topped centre table, made circa 1890. Although this attempts to be very rococo it is too stiff and symmetrical. It is strange that at the same time that the asymmetrical art nouveau was current, the popularist antique styles were so rigid and insisted on symmetrical interpretations of an asymmetrical style – for the original rococo was orderly but asymmetrical.

Below: Now we move into the later part of the 1890s. This bed in kingwood *au soleil* (veneered in 'ray' pattern) is embellished with gilt-brass foliage that is almost art nouveau in design.

Above: A pair of cabinets with curved glass. They are in the grand late 19th-century Parisian style with marble tops, curved glass doors, and almost every available space encrusted in gilt-brass 'enrichments'.

Above: From the same period is a kingwood vitrine with gilt-brass mounts. The base is slightly bombé (outwardly curved in the vertical and horizontal planes). These vitrines often have curved glass, which is incredibly fragile. This example has a marble top – this construction often confuses house removers, with the result that the marble crashes to the floor! The backboard is covered in watered silk.

Above: This final item of Continental furniture is substantial: a grand piano. The case and the gilt-brass mounts were made by François Linke (1855–1946), the premier Parisian ébéniste at the end of the 19th century. He received a gold medal at the Exposition Universelle in 1900. Linke was a very commercial maker. He had several shops and produced photographic catalogues of room settings that were entirely furnished with his own productions. He worked in a very freely interpreted version of the Louis XV style but brought that style into the 20th century so successfully that his furniture is faithfully copied today. Sadly, today's makers do not have the quality of casting and chasing that Linke was able to use. The man-hours involved in the fine finishing of the mounts would be prohibitive at today's rates.

ENGLISH CHAIRS
1837 – 1900

The Victorian period saw the change from classical designs in the 1840s to Arts and Crafts in the later part of the century, and even the start of modernism with bentwood, metal, and 'engineered' chairs at the beginning of the 20th century. The search for new ideas in both design and construction, which itself led to several dead ends, produced so many objects that a simplified overview is almost impossible. This article is restricted to those chairs that have appeared in Sotheby's auction galleries in London.

Left: This is a Victorian interpretation, circa 1840, of a George II shepherd's-crook armchair. It might be confused with a German chair because it has strange Baroque-influenced arms and back. However, the construction is English (glued, not pegged) and the size and angle of the back legs is typically English.

Right: The two armchairs shown here would originally have been covered in fabric. They date from the middle of the century and are wide and comfortable. Although not very exaggerated in these particular chairs, the front supports for the arms had to be taken as far towards the back of the chair as possible to accommodate the full skirts of Victorian fashion – the chair shown above would have been of little use to a Victorian lady!

Above: This is a Victorian copy of a Chippendale-style chair from the 1760s. I include it because many very good copies of Georgian chairs were made in the 19th century. Often the only way to tell them apart is that they are too good – too clean and crisp, and slightly too well constructed. This may sound odd, but it should be remembered that the Victorians liked precision engineering, and believed that their woodwork should be as precise as their engineering. Perfectly made joints can often be a sign of 19th-century origin. This is a very beautiful chair and in 200 years' time it won't matter much whether it was made by hand in 1760 or 1860.

Above: Here is a more typical Victorian walnut dining chair. A drawing-room chair would probably have less padding at the back and some carved decoration on the lower part of the oval back. Dining-room chairs were made more comfortable and of larger section timbers than drawing-room standard chairs. ('Standard chair' is the term used for a chair without arms when it is not around a dining table.) This chair is in the 'naturalistic' style, that is with leaf and scroll carving, cabochon ornament and slender cabriole legs. The carved faces are rather unusual. The chair is somewhat Louis XV in style, and dates from the middle of the 19th century.

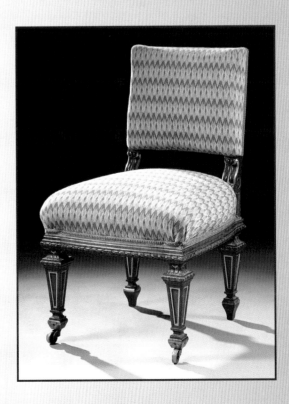

Right: I'm afraid that in 200 years' time no one will care much about the type of chair shown here. It was made around 1860 by a prestigious firm – Holland & Sons. It is of walnut and parcel-gilt in a retrospective style, a cross between Elizabethan and Renaissance. The seat is rounded at the edges and very thick – partly because springs are now being used in upholstery, and partly because of the greater availability and width of covering fabric. Upholsterers no longer had to be parsimonious about the height of the seat above the tacking rail. These chairs are almost stools with added backrests. One cannot deny that they are very well made, but they are not attractive. Large, heavy chairs and settees are usually 19th-century.

Above: Now we move to more familiar shapes. The two chairs shown here both date from the 1880s. The one on the left was made by a famous name in the furniture trade: James Schoolbred. The one on the right was made by Howard & Sons. In the later years of the century 'easy chairs', as we would call them, were born. The seats were lower to the ground, sometimes open below the arms, sometimes with a fully upholstered scrolled-over arm. In the 1880s they usually had turned feet. Often the feet are the only pieces of timber that you can see, so it is necessary to learn to tell the age of a chair from the foot and the castor.

Below: The two chairs shown below are in Louis XVI style, circa 1880. These are simply blatant copies of the French originals, but in rosewood. The originals would have been in beech and gilded, or perhaps in mahogany and polished.

Above: More copies of French chairs are shown here. These two, from a set, are in rather a hotchpotch style, part Louis XIV, part 'Elizabethan'. The joinery is too good to be truly 18th-century or earlier, notwithstanding the ponderous decoration which is derived from earlier pieces.

Below: The final photograph shows another 'revival' chair, this time from the Regency Revival. In fact the painted decoration and the caning on this chair is very fine, but the chair does date from the early years of the 20th century.

Above: This pair of satinwood dining chairs dates from around 1905. They are shield-back chairs in the Sheraton style. As with carcass furniture, the Edwardian period was the last time when chairs were made, in any large numbers, using traditional techniques. These look much like the late 18th-century originals but the sections of timber are not quite so delicate and the sense of gracefulness is missing from the backs.

I cannot close without mentioning one of the major inventions of the 19th century – the bentwood chair. They are so well known that no illustration is necessary. Michael Thonet introduced bentwood furniture to England in the Great Exhibition of 1851 in London.

CONTINENTAL CHAIRS
1850 – 1900

On the Continent, from 1850 to 1900, chairs continued to emulate grand designs from the past. But by 1890, style-setters in Britain were switching their affections to art nouveau.

Left: The first photograph shows a fine carved oak Venetian armchair, circa 1860. The carving is in the 17th-century manner after Andrea Brustolon (b. 1662). The figures sitting on the back of the arms are cherubs and the front supports are Moors. This is an example of the 'historical' style of chair.

Above: A boulle salon suite. The chairs are boulle and contre-boulle. This means that the two skins of brass and tortoiseshell have been swapped over on each chair – what was brass on the right-hand chair is tortoiseshell on the left-hand one and vice-versa. The brass inlay and the faces on the canapé are typical of the original boulle period, circa 1700.

Above: A French canapé, circa 1870. This is gilt wood in Louis XVI style. The art of chair making never really died out in France and such frames are still being made today. The covering is silk damask.

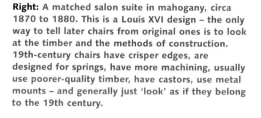

Above: Another carved Italian chair is shown here. This throne-like chair was made around 1870 and has carved gilt wood surmounted by cherubs, on boldly scrolled legs and claw feet. The Italians had a very bold and vibrant style of carving. Although this piece is 19th-century, the motifs have their origins in much earlier times.

Right: A matched salon suite in mahogany, circa 1870 to 1880. This is a Louis XVI design – the only way to tell later chairs from original ones is to look at the timber and the methods of construction. 19th-century chairs have crisper edges, are designed for springs, have more machining, usually use poorer-quality timber, have castors, use metal mounts – and generally just 'look' as if they belong to the 19th century.

Left: Now here is something different. This is an Italian grotto suite, circa 1880. The shell-like chairs are made for use in a grotto or other garden setting. These are carved, painted, silvered and parcel-gilt. When you consider the limitations of animal glue, which is what was used, it is remarkable that these chairs have survived. Perhaps it is down to careful timber selection and jointing. However, the garden for which they were made probably had lots of under-gardeners to carry them in out of the damp.

Left: Here is another pair of Italian 'Renaissance' chairs, circa 1880. They are part ebony and part ebonized. The backs are set with hard stones and inlaid with tortoiseshell. The central panel is of ivory, engraved with figures after the Italian painter Salvatore Rosa (1615–73). The seats are similarly decorated.

Above: This French salon suite was made in about 1880 from carved and gilded beech in Louis XVI style. The same remarks that I made earlier regarding the differentiation between 18th-century originals and 19th-century copies apply here. In the 19th century, making copies using traditional methods was not regarded as 'faking', as we might consider it today. This suite was made in the spirit of acceptance and acknowledgement that the design and the techniques were good and were worth preserving. Such techniques are still preserved, and taught today in French furniture colleges. Their students are not urged to search for new seating designs. They are first taught the traditional methods, including how to use and properly sharpen hand tools. The result appears to be that the French have a very good and healthy hand-made furniture tradition. At the École Boulle in Paris, before students learn how to cut marquetry (using piercing saw blades that they make themselves), they spend an entire year learning how to make traditional chairs by hand.

Above: Here is a French gilt-bronze and mahogany salon suite in Empire style, circa 1880. Once again this pays homage to an earlier style, relying on the inspiration of Jacob and Desmalter (see pages 128–131).

Right: An example of the ubiquitous Aubusson suite. Aubusson is a town in France that has given its name to a type of tapestry. In tapestry, as opposed to needlepoint or embroidery, the pattern is woven on a loom as part of the fabric, so the picture is made within the fabric, not applied to it. Tapestries had been made at Aubusson on handlooms for hundreds of years, but the tapestries shown here are made with the aid of machines. The resultant reduction in manufacturing costs meant that tapestry, once the preserve of royalty and aristocrats, could be applied to furniture made for the middle classes. These frames are made in a vaguely 18th-century style, are badly carved and badly gilded, and have mass-produced tapestries fitted. They are really the epitome of the nadir of the French furniture trade.

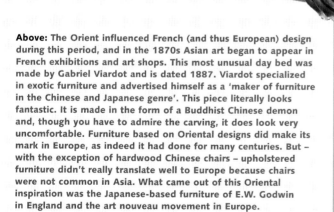

Above: The Orient influenced French (and thus European) design during this period, and in the 1870s Asian art began to appear in French exhibitions and art shops. This most unusual day bed was made by Gabriel Viardot and is dated 1887. Viardot specialized in exotic furniture and advertised himself as a 'maker of furniture in the Chinese and Japanese genre'. This piece literally looks fantastic. It is made in the form of a Buddhist Chinese demon and, though you have to admire the carving, it does look very uncomfortable. Furniture based on Oriental designs did make its mark in Europe, as indeed it had done for many centuries. But – with the exception of hardwood Chinese chairs – upholstered furniture didn't really translate well to Europe because chairs were not common in Asia. What came out of this Oriental inspiration was the Japanese-based furniture of E.W. Godwin in England and the art nouveau movement in Europe.

Right: These bergères are as poorly made as the suite shown at top right. They are vaguely in Empire style, but the carved faces of the caryatids supporting the arms are third-rate. Again, a great design has become debased. Don't forget, though, that in 1890, when these were made, the rich and famous were not buying Empire and Louis XVI furniture – they were buying art nouveau.

ENGLISH MIRRORS

In 1664 the Worshipful Company of Glass-Sellers and Looking Glass Makers was formed. Even at that date glass was a rare commodity. However, as the 18th century progressed, glass became more and more accessible for furniture-makers to use. The subject of mirrors is dealt with comprehensively in Graham Child's book, *World Mirrors*. The subject of mirrors is huge – and this is only a small selection of fine examples.

Above: First we have two dressing-table mirrors, circa 1710. The bodies of both mirror stands have been japanned (that is, the makers used European varnishes to produce a finish that looks superficially like Oriental lacquer) in black and gilt. These small Queen Anne mirrors were great treasures for bedrooms and contained a miniature bureau base for valuables and favourite things such as letters and jewellery. The marks on the back of the left-hand mirror glass are normal and acceptable signs of age. In those days the silvering on a mirror was formed using mercury. Over time the silvering has deteriorated and the surface now has black spots, missing and flaking silvering. Nothing can be done to correct these marks: they are legitimate signs of age and it would be quite wrong to try to resilver the mirror. It would be acceptable to remove the glass and put modern glass in, provided the old glass were safely stored away and kept. If the mirror ever comes to be sold it will be worth much more with the original glass, than with replacement glass, even though the reflective quality of new glass is much better.

Above: This mirror dates from 1740. It is a walnut-framed George II mirror in what is known as a 'cut-card' frame. The scrolled fretwork has the outline of card cut with a decorative scrolled edge. The term is borrowed from silversmiths, who used similar decoration. The scrolls at the sides are called 'ears' and the groundwork is usually pine. Many of these mirrors were made in the 18th, 19th and even the 20th centuries. They are very easily faked, so beware. Old glass is thin and has many irregularities and is about ⅛in (3mm) thick, while modern glass is absolutely flat and is of uniform thickness – usually ⁵⁄₃₂in (4mm) plate. Another sign of age is the bevel, if present. In general, old bevels are very wide and slightly irregular, whereas modern bevels are narrow and precise.

Below: This is a very rare mirror containing a Chinese reverse-painted glass. It was made in about 1760. The glass was painted in China and then mounted in a rococo frame that was carved and gilded in England. This particular mirror achieved the world-record price for its type: £298,500 (US$534,790). Unusually, the back boards were held together in their length by tiny bamboo dowels, indicating that either a Chinese craftsman was working in the place where it was assembled or that English woodworkers had been taught to use Chinese techniques and materials. The backboards would normally be rub-jointed together and held in place by panel pins or sprigs in the side rebate. The joints would then have brown tape gummed over them to prevent the entry of dust. The decoration is ornamented with carved bells, phoenixes and icicles. The carving is a mid-Georgian flamboyant fantasy, 6ft (1.83m) high.

Far left: Here is a simpler glass. This one is a fairly conventional Georgian oval mirror, 2ft 9in (838mm) high, with original glass, contained in a gadroon-carved frame surrounded by scrolls and surmounted with cresting carved with a plume and scroll.

Left: This is a fake Georgian mirror of a similar style to the one above. The carving is too symmetrical and has a kind of Victorian neatness about it. Georgian carving was more undercut, but there is a simpler way to tell that this is a fake. The central panel of glass extends under the carving in some places and the gilded edges are laid on top of the glass. Glass was so precious and difficult to cut to shape that this trick was not used in the 18th century. The curved panels of glass were kept small in case they broke as they were cut – that way only a small amount of glass was lost. By the following century glass was less precious and more risks were taken with the cutting. Glass could also be manufactured in larger sheets.

Above: A selection of three Georgian dressing mirrors is shown here. The oval dressing-table mirror dates from about 1785. It has ivory paterae, knobs and escutcheon. The rectangular dressing-table mirror was made about 1810. It is veneered in good-quality flared mahogany, has ivory embellishments and has a boxwood lattice inlay to the sides of the drawer compartment. The rectangular wall-glass is also circa 1810, and was probably mounted in a gentleman's dressing room in such a position that it could be used for shaving. Once again it has ivory decoration.

Left: A gilt wood convex Regency mirror, circa 1815, is shown next. Circular convex mirrors became extremely popular in the Regency period and they are one of the 'standard issue' furniture items of this period. The same design elements tended to be included on all convex mirrors. They had a domed glass, giving a widened view of the room, a reeded and ebonized slip surrounding the glass, a ring of spherical balls inside the frame and a substantial surmount – in this case an eagle perched on a shell.

Right: Another variant of the pattern is shown here. The thin wire scroll candle arms are covered in compo and gesso and then gilded. Another name for a mirror with candle arms is a 'girandole'.

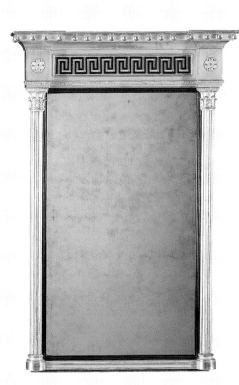

Above: This rectangular mirror is from the Regency period. It conforms to the classical architectural pattern with cornice and columns. Note that the cornice has spherical ball beading, like the convex mirrors. The frieze is decorated with an ebonized Greek-key pattern.

Right: This is an early 19th-century copy of a Chippendale-style mirror. Although the frame contains the standard rococo elements, such as trailing foliage, 'C' scrolls and even a 'surmount' in the form of a rocky outcrop, the designer was unable to make the whole thing appear naturally asymmetrical. This is a 19th-century interpretation of naturalistic carving, in which nature has been made to conform to geometry. Compare the opposite sides of the 1760 mirror shown on page 205: in that case the scrolls and the foliage, although balanced, are very slightly different on each side.

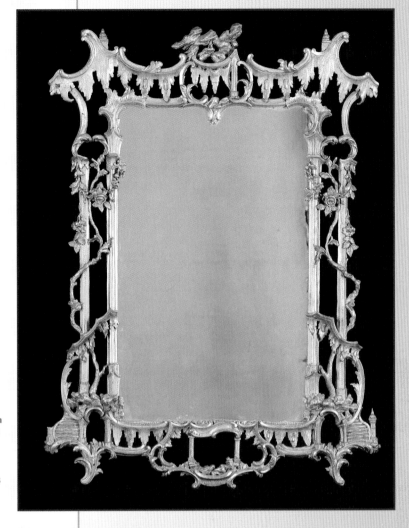

Below: Finally, we have a pair of Victorian dressing-table mirrors in mahogany, made circa 1850. Like the first mirrors on page 204, these have a drawer in the base for 'favourite things'. The scrolled supports at the sides are called 'horns'. The horns frequently become loose, due to the small joint between the horn and the base, which has to take the weight of the top-heavy mirror above. The brass swivel fittings also become worn. Wherever possible, keep the original brass fittings and have them repaired rather than replaced.

CONTINENTAL MIRRORS PART I

There was a wider range of mirror shapes on the Continent than in Britain, with the result that there are more mirrors to study. Late 17th- and early 18th-century frames were predominantly 'simple' in form. I use inverted commas because some of the constructional methods were far from simple, but the overall impression is of a less complex design than those in use in later times.

Left: The first photograph shows a 17th-century Flemish frame with a ripple-cut and waved border. The timber is ebonized and is likely to be pear. Solid ebony was also used, but was much more expensive. The size is 2ft 9in x 3ft 2in (838 x 965mm) overall. At this date, the measuring system used on the Continent was based on the pied (French for 'foot') and the subdivisions were twelfths of a pied. The actual size of a pied was only about $^{13}/_{64}$in (5.2mm) larger than a British foot, so the basic unit of design at this time, and for many years to come, was closer to the British foot than to any increment of a metre. So, for historical study, it is helpful to be able to visualize in a dodecagonal system.

Right: The second mirror shown is Italian, again from the 17th century. It is 2ft x 1ft 9in (610 x 533mm). The substrate is pine, with gilt metal panels between ebonized mouldings.

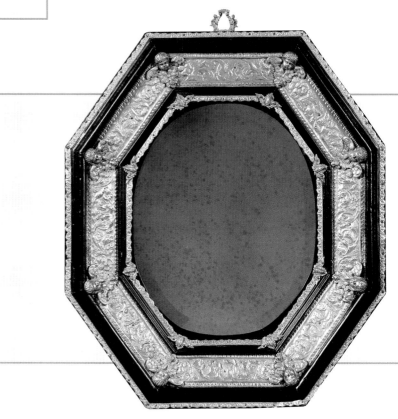

Left and below: These frames are Spanish, made around 1700. They are boldly carved acanthus leaves, which have been gilded overall, 2ft 4in x 2ft 1in (711 x 635mm). These are almost certainly frames for miniatures that have subsequently had mirror glass put in them. Note the darkening to the gilding at the bottom scroll and the overhanging crest above. This is probably smoke damage, caused because they were hung near a fire.

Above: This is a splendid Venetian mirror dating from about 1700. The frame has been varnished with a dark brown 'lacquer' (not a true Oriental lacquer) and painted with foliage trails, the petals of which are inlaid in mother-of-pearl. The corners and central crest have faux tortoiseshell bosses and the frame is enriched with carved and gilded acanthus leaf scrolls. It is 5ft 5in x 3ft 11in (1651 x 1194mm). This brown lacquer technique is rare, and the whole effect makes a very striking mirror. Sadly, the original glass has now lost its silvering, but the value of the whole item would be severely reduced if the original glass were removed. If modern glass is to be put in then the original should be carefully kept – I cannot repeat this advice often enough. Enormous amounts of damage have been done to historic objects because some well-meaning person has 'improved' them.

Left: This is a Flemish frame covered in red tortoiseshell, dating from the second half of the 17th century. The simple cross-section is known as 'cushion moulding'. Between and bordering the 'cushions' are ripple mouldings, the innermost of which has been ebonized. The size is 4ft x 3ft 3in (1219 x 991mm).

Left: This Dutch walnut-framed mirror measures 5ft 5in x 3ft 5in (1651 x 1041mm). It dates from the late 17th or early 18th century. The plain frame is now beginning to have substantial ornament attached to it in the form of a pierced, carved and gilded cresting.

Right: A Flemish frame is shown next. This is a carved wooden frame, but is deeply undercut and gilded. Because of the labour involved, deep undercutting does not usually appear on later objects. If you see a process which is labour-intensive on an object it probably indicates that the object was made prior to 1800. This frame dates from the first half of the 17th century. This frame measures 5ft x 3ft 10in (1524 x 1168mm), which is a lot of carving!

Right: The next two mirrors are Spanish. The first is a carved mirror, 4ft 2in x 3ft 4in (1270 x 1016mm), made around 1720. Spanish decoration was much bolder than northern European decoration. The Spanish were not shy and liked their scrolls to be noticeable, as this mirror with 4ft-long sides demonstrates. Once again the glass is old and should be kept with the mirror.

Above: The second Spanish mirror is a rare example from the first half of the 18th century. It is 4ft 6in x 3ft 7in (1372 x 1092mm). The polygonal decoration is the result of the Moorish influence on Spanish art.

Right: Finally we move into the 18th century proper, with a Venetian mirror, 6ft 5in x 4ft 5in (1956 x 1346mm), made around 1730. This mirror moves away from the concept of a mirror frame being a glorified picture frame. This mirror is proud of itself, the mirror frame has become an artistic object in its own right. There are scrolls, swags, trellis work and vases. Mirrors have become an architectural statement in miniature.

CONTINENTAL
MIRRORS PART II

Left: By the 1750s quite large sheets of glass were being produced, which meant that many mirrors were becoming quite substantial in size. A case in point is this frame from Genoa, made around 1750, which is 9ft 7in (2.92m) high and 6ft 2in (1.88mm) wide. This example is so large that it is intended to rest on the floor.

Below: Not all designs were huge, however, and in complete contrast we have here a pair of Lombardo-Veneto girandoles, made sometime in the mid 18th century. Girandoles are mirrors designed to reflect candle light from a candle-arm attached to the mirror surround. These have a single sconce, whereas other designs often feature two sconces. The frames are heavily ornamented with leaves, flowers and rocaille, the stylized rockwork associated with rococo decoration.

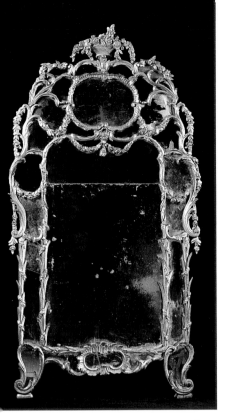

Left: Here we have a complex frame dating from 1750, probably made in Piedmont. The divisions of the frame are formed as bulrushes and swags of flowers. The frame is large, some 8ft 10in x 3ft 10in (2.69 x 1.17m). The mirror glass would have been sub-divided according to the frame. The large glass in the centre would probably have been one sheet, although sometimes two cleanly cut sheets were butted up to each other. Damaged or altered mirrors often had the join between plates covered with a gilded moulding that doesn't match any other part of the decoration. It is not untypical for the moulding to have been 'planted on'.

Above: Next we have a pair of engraved mirrors. Once again they are Venetian. Venice was one of the big centres for objects using glass, particularly coloured and engraved glass. These two mirrors have Japanned frames and are 18th-century. The top mirror features a satyr – a mythological attendant of Bacchus with hairy goat-like legs, tail and hooves – while the bottom one has a figure in a pastoral landscape. The allusions to Bacchus and romantic landscapes are an 18th-century riposte to the sober clarity of 'reason' as represented in Classical Greek thought and art.

Left: Once mirrors had established their importance in decorative schemes, they didn't have to be large and showy (although up to and beyond the 19th century some clients continued to want them that way). Here we have a set of six small Venetian mirrors, measuring 2ft 5in x 1ft 5in (737 x 432mm). Made in about 1750, they have delicately painted frames and engraved glasses. As you can see, they are for ornamental purposes and not for looking into. The engravings are of Bacchic figures (worshippers of Bacchus, the god of wine). Unfortunately, two of the original plates are missing.

Above: Reverting to the more mundane, these Italian mirrors date from about 1780. The crowns of flowers at the top enclose ears of corn. These are formed by moulding compo and gesso around metal wires. The bigger objects, such as the actual ears of corn, are first formed in moulds and then glued to the metal wires. Once the wire gets distorted and the gesso or compo cracks, it is very hard to repair the damage invisibly without major work.

Above: This is one of a pair of finely carved Tuscan mirrors, from around 1780, measuring some 8ft 4in x 3ft 10in (2.54 x 1.17m). This is certainly a frame that deserves a close examination, as it features some of the best examples of multiple-element carved decoration I have ever seen. Almost every design feature is included, but the entirety is not overcrowded. There is an obvious similarity to English neo-classical mirrors from the same date. The central vase is supported by acanthus leaves which, as the eye progresses down, turn into Greek-key designs. To either side are female griffins (head, wings and claws of an eagle with the body of a lion) terminating in scrolling foliage. Below all this is a classical four-element frieze. At the bottom are swags and brackets, centred by a medallion formed by entwined serpents, enclosing a view of a tree-lined avenue. In this instance the glass plates are divided intentionally, because the mirror is so tall.

Above and opposite page: By the late 18th century some mirror frames were becoming simpler again, such as these two Venetian mirrors made around 1790. The decoration comprises subdued painting and gilding.

Left: The painting on the mirror shown here is rather attractive. The arched cresting has a little scene of a lion in a landscape surmounted by a stylized scallop shell, while the sides and base have a running border formed of a single vine hung with leaves and bunches of grapes. The mirror is Italian and was made around 1800.

Below: We move into the early part of the 19th century with this rectangular Venetian blue glass mirror. Reminiscent of the simple rectangular mirrors that we started with in the late 17th century, the glass slips are cut as rhomboids to give an effect of perspective. This is a far cry from the beautifully elegant mirrors of the middle of the previous century shown on the opposite page. These 19th-century mirrors were undoubtedly significantly cheaper to make and were produced in much larger numbers.

SELECTIVE GLOSSARY OF FURNITURE TERMS

armoire French term for a cupboard.

banquette a window seat with raised ends but no back.

bead a small raised moulding.

bellflower a carved ornament representing a bell-shaped flower.

bergère an armchair with enclosed, upholstered sides.

bibliothèque French term for a bookcase.

board archaic term for a table.

bois clair any pale-coloured wood.

bole a clay-based preparation used as a ground for gilding.

bombé having surfaces which are convex in both vertical and horizontal directions.

bonheur-du-jour a small writing desk with a superstructure of shelves, cupboard or tambour.

bookmatching the technique of laying two consecutive sheets of veneer side by side so that the figure forms a mirror image.

boulle a form of marquetry using brass and tortoiseshell.

bow front a convex front to a piece of furniture.

bracket foot a foot on a piece of case furniture, formed from two pieces of wood joined at right angles to give an L shape in plan view.

break-front cabinet a cabinet in which the centre section projects forward of the sides.

broken pediment a pediment with a gap in the middle.

brushing slide a flat, pull-out slide, sometimes covered in baize, on which clothes may be laid for brushing.

buffet in medieval times, a multi-tiered structure for displaying plate; in Victorian times, a serving table.

bun foot a turned foot of spherical or flattened spherical shape.

bureau à cylindre a desk whose lid is in the shape of a quarter-cylinder.

bureau-bookcase a desk whose upper part forms an enclosed bookcase.

bureau de dame a small desk for ladies.

bureau-plat a desk consisting of a flat-topped table with drawers in the apron.

burr an abnormal growth on a tree, with convoluted grain from which highly decorative veneers can be made.

butler's tray a try with hinged sides that can be let down to form a flat surface.

cabling a carved ornament imitating twisted rope.

cabriole leg a furniture leg whose profile curves outward to form a 'knee' at the top, balanced by a reverse curve lower down.

cache-pot a plant-pot holder.

canapé French term for a small settee or sofa.

canterbury a small stand with partitions for sheet music or magazines (illustrated p. 159).

carton-pierre a material resembling papier mâché but strengthened with additional ingredients, used to make moulded ornament.

cartouche a tablet or panel with scrolled edges.

caryatid a support in the form of a whole or partial female figure.

cassone Italian term for a chest, especially an ornate one.

cellarette a wine-cooler.

chest-on-chest a tall chest of drawers made in two sections, one above the other.

chest-on-stand a cabinet or chest of drawers mounted on a table-like stand.

cheval mirror a large mirror pivoting within a free-standing frame (illustrated p. 126).

chiffonier Victorian term for a small, low cabinet, usually with two doors, intended to stand against a wall.

chinoiserie a Western decorative style involving fanciful imitation of Chinese motifs.

chip carving decorative carving consisting of incised geometrical shapes.

claw-and-ball (or **ball-and-claw**) **foot** a foot carved to resemble animal or bird claws gripping a ball.

close nailing a style of upholstery in which large decorative nails are closely spaced, usually touching, around the edges.

commode French term for a chest of drawers.

compo short for 'composition': a preparation of chalk, glue and other ingredients used to make moulded decoration.

console-desserte a marble-topped table with shelf below, to stand against a wall.

console table a table that is attached to the wall and not free-standing.

contre-boulle a piece of boulle marquetry in which the materials of design and ground are reversed.

corner-chair a chair with a low back around two adjacent sides.

court-cupboard a sideboard of the 16th or 17th century, typically with an enclosed upper storey and open lower part.

credenza Victorian term for a low cabinet, usually of serpentine form with an enclosed central section and curved, often glazed doors at the ends.

crest rail the uppermost back rail of a chair or settee.

cross-banding a band of contrasting veneer around the edge of a veneered surface, with its grain perpendicular to the edges of the surface.

dais the platform on which the high table stands in a medieval hall.

damask a luxurious woven fabric with a raised pattern.

davenport a compact desk with sloping top and drawers opening to the side (illustrated p. 117).

dentils a row of small square blocks in a Classical entablature, above the frieze and below the cornice (illustrated p. 89).

double knife-cut veneer machine-cut veneer approx. 0.05in (1.2mm) thick.

dresser a name given to various forms of side table, either for serving food or for storing plate and utensils.

drop-in seat an upholstered seat for a chair or settee, made separately and inserted into a recess in the frame.

dumb waiter a stand for serving food, comprising several trays mounted one above the other.

ébéniste French term for a superior cabinetmaker, originally referring to the use of ebony veneer.

ebonizing a process of staining and polishing wood to imitate ebony.

egg-and-dart a carved ornament consisting of alternating egg-like and pointed shapes running along an ovolo (quarter-round) moulding.

entablature in Classical architecture, the whole of the horizontal assembly that rests on the columns.

escutcheon a protective and ornamental mount around a keyhole.

fasces a bundle of rods from which an axe blade protrudes, used by the Romans as a symbol of authority.

fauteuil an upholstered armchair with open sides (also the ordinary word for an armchair in modern French).

figure any decorative pattern appearing on the surface of wood as a result of the grain configuration and other natural features.

fluting a series of parallel semicircular grooves used as a decorative element.

frieze a long, narrow panel forming the main horizontal element of the Classical entablature, or a furniture part resembling this.

gadrooning carved ornament consisting of repeated convex teardrop-like lobes along the edge of a projecting member.

gallery a railing, usually brass, around the edge of a desktop or shelf.

gesso a preparation of whiting and animal glue, used as a ground for painting or gilding.

girandole a mirror with one or more candleholders attached.

golden mean a system of proportion favoured in Classical architecture, in which a line or area is divided so that the ratio of the smaller part to the larger equals the ratio of the larger part to the whole.

Greek key an ornamental band or meander composed of right-angled elements.

guéridon table a small table with tripod base.

guilloche a carved ornament comprising a row of circles outlined by interlacing bands.

hall chair a chair having the general form of a dining chair, but made entirely of wood, without upholstery (illustrated p. 145).

hall stand a tall stand for coats, sticks and umbrellas (illustrated p. 161).

harewood a pale wood, usually European sycamore (*Acer pseudoplatanus*), originally stained green but subsequently fading to grey.

intarsia a pictorial design made up from pieces of contrasting woods or other materials, generally thicker than ordinary marquetry.

japanning a varnished finish used in the West to simulate Oriental lacquer.

jardinière a plant stand or holder.

joint stool a robust stool with splayed legs, assembled with mortice and tenon joints, characteristic of the Tudor period.

klismos a lightly built chair with sabre legs, originating in ancient Greece and imitated by neo-classical designers (illustrated p. 13).

kneehole desk a desk with drawers or cupboards either side of a recessed area to accommodate the user's knees.

Knole settee a settee of 17th-century form with end panels supported by decorative tassels (illustrated p. 35).

lacewood plane wood (*Platanus* sp.) with a distinctive flecked figure.

lacquer an extremely durable coloured finish containing sap from the lacquer tree, *Rhus verniciflua*, developed in the Orient and much imitated in the West.

library chair Victorian term for a heavily upholstered armchair, regarded as a characteristically 'masculine' item.

library table a centre table constructed to support heavy books.

linenfold a medieval style of carving in which the surface is grooved to resemble hanging cloth.

loo table a small circular or oval table for card-playing (illustrated p. 158).

marquetry a pictorial design made up from pieces of contrasting woods or other materials, generally thinner than intarsia.

Mazarin bureau a flat-topped desk with eight legs and two or three tiers of drawers.

méridienne a short sofa with ends but no back.

metamorphic furniture convertible furniture, such as a chair which unfolds to become library steps.

meuble d'appui a low storage cupboard, placed against a wall.

nulling a variety of gadrooning in which the lobes are alternately concave and convex.

oil-gilding the process of laying gold leaf using gold-size.

ormolu brass or bronze gilded by a mercury or electro-gilding process, used for furniture mounts.

ottoman an upholstered couch without arms or back, often with storage inside.

overstuffed heavily upholstered, with the outer covering nailed to the outside of the frame.

pad foot a rounded, flattened foot.

parcel-gilding gilding applied to certain parts of an article, rather than all over.

partners' desk a large desk at which two people can sit opposite one another.

patera (pl. **paterae**) a decorative rosette.

patina tarnish on a metal or other surface, especially when regarded as an attractive feature.

pedestal an enclosed square stand, often surmounted by an urn; a forerunner of the sideboard.

pedestal table a table with a single central support.

pediment a shallow triangular gable in Classical architecture.

pegged joint a joint that is secured by a wooden peg passing through the tenon and both cheeks of the mortice.

Pembroke table a small rectangular table with hinged leaves on the long sides (illustrated p. 91).

pen-engraving decoration of incised lines, usually filled with black wax, in a calligraphic style.

penwork a type of decoration in which fine details are executed in a calligraphic style, sometimes actually using pen and ink.

pie-crust edging a carved, scalloped edging to a tray or table top.

pied a former French measurement, slightly larger than the British foot.

pier table a table intended to stand against the wall between two windows.

pietre-dure a form of marquetry using different-coloured stones.

pilaster a flattened column.

plate cupboard another term for a buffet, in the medieval sense.

plinth the square base of a column, or of a piece of carcass furniture.

plum-pudding veneer veneer with a distinctive mottled figure.

pollard a tree whose branches have been repeatedly cut back to around head-height, forming a burr-like growth with convoluted grain.

press an archaic term for a cupboard.

prie-dieu chair a chair with a low seat and tall back, on which one may kneel to pray.

reeding ornament comprising a series of parallel half-round mouldings.

ripple a type of figure in wood, in which undulating grain gives rise to prominent stripes of different reflectivity at right angles to the grain.

ripple moulding a moulding, typically in ebony, decorated with a regular pattern of transverse waves or ripples (illustrated p. 208).

riven timber wood that is cleft rather than sawn to size.

rule joint a joint used in drop-leaf tables, comprising a convex edge on the fixed leaf mating with a concave edge on the drop leaf so that no gap appears when the leaf is dropped.

sabot a metal mount enclosing the bottom of a furniture leg.

sabre leg a leg with a gentle curve throughout its length, like that of a sabre.

salon suite a suite of upholstered furniture for the drawing room, comprising as many as 10 or 11 pieces.

seaweed marquetry a style of marquetry using delicate interlacing tendrils, originating in the Netherlands and fashionable in England c.1700.

secrétaire à abattant a desk with a pull-down front.

serpentine undulating in shape.

serving table a side table for serving food.

show wood exposed wood on an upholstered piece of furniture.

single knife-cut veneer machine-cut veneer around 0.025in (0.6mm) thick.

slab a furniture component made from a single wide piece of wood, as opposed to a constructed frame and panel.

sofa table a narrow, rectangular table with drop leaves at the ends, and drawers (illustrated p. 110).

spade foot a square, tapered foot, resembling a blunt arrowhead.

spalting a fungal discoloration in wood, sometimes used as a decorative feature.

spandrel a triangular shape with two straight and one concave sides, such as the space left between an arch and its rectangular surround.

specimen table a style of table which makes decorative use of contrasting materials.

splat the broad central upright in certain types of chair back.

squab cushion a removable cushion for a chair or settee.

strapwork relief-carved ornament resembling straps or ribbons.

table à écrire a lady's small writing table with drawers.

tacking rail the rail surrounding the seat in a chair or settee, to which the upholstery is nailed.

tallboy another term for chest-on-chest.

tambour a flexible shutter made of wooden slats.

term a support in the form of a partial human figure.

torchère French term for a candle stand.

toupie foot a foot in the shape of a spinning top.

verre églomisé glass decorated with engraved gold leaf on the reverse.

vitrine a glazed display cabinet.

what-not Victorian term for a set of shelves.

window seat another name for a banquette.

FURTHER READING

Aldrich, Megan *Gothic Revival* (London: Phaidon, 1994)

Aronson, Joseph *The Encyclopaedia of Furniture* (New York: Crown, 1938)

Burkett, Mary E. *The Furniture of Gillow of Lancaster* (Lancaster City Art Gallery, 1969)

Cescinsky, Herbert *The Gentle Art of Faking Furniture* (London: Chapman & Hall, 1931)

Child, Graham *World Mirrors 1650–1900* (London: Sotheby's, 1990)

Chinnery, Victor *Oak Furniture: The British Tradition* (Woodbridge, Suffolk: Antique Collectors' Club, 1979)

Chippendale, Thomas *The Gentleman and Cabinet Maker's Director,* 3rd edn (1762; repr. NewYork: Dover, 1966)

Collard, Frances *Regency Furniture* (Woodbridge, Suffolk: Antique Collectors' Club, 1985)

Cooper, Jeremy *Victorian and Edwardian Furniture and Interiors from the Gothic Revival to Art Nouveau* (London: Thames & Hudson, 1987)

Edwards, Clive D. *Encyclopaedia of Furniture Making Materials, Trades and Techniques* (Aldershot: Ashgate, 2001)

Edwards, Ralph *The Shorter Dictionary of English Furniture,* rev. edn (London: Country Life, 1964)

Gloag, John *Dictionary of Furniture,* rev. Clive Edwards (London: Unwin Hyman, 1990)

—— *A Social History of Furniture Design from BC 1300 to AD 1960* (London: Cassell, 1966)

Hamilton Jackson, Frederick *Intarsia and Marquetry* (n. pl.: Sands, 1903)

Hayward, Charles *Antique or Fake? The Making of Old Furniture* (London: Evans Bros., 1970)

Hayward, Helena (ed.) *World Furniture: An Illustrated History from Earliest Times* (London: Hamlyn, 1965)

Hepplewhite, George *The Cabinet-Maker & Upholsterer's Guide,* 3rd edn (1794; repr. New York: Dover, 1969)

Jekyll, Gertrude, and Jones, Sydney *Old English Household Life* (London: Batsford, 1925)

Jervis, Simon *Victorian Furniture* (London: Ward Lock, 1968)

Jourdain, Margaret *Regency Furniture 1795–1820,* rev. Ralph Fastnedge (London: Country Life, 1965)

Joy, Edward T. *English Furniture 1800–1851* (London: Ward Lock/Sotheby's, 1977)

Macquoid, Percy *A History of English Furniture* (1904–8; repr. London: Bracken Books, 1989)

—— **and Edwards, Ralph** *The Dictionary of English Furniture from the Middle Ages to the Late Georgian Period,* 3 vols., rev. Ralph Edwards (Woodbridge, Suffolk: Antique Collectors' Club, 2000)

Musgrave, Clifford *Regency Furniture 1800–1830,* 2nd edn (London: Faber, 1970)

Oates, Phyllis Bennett *The Story of Western Furniture* (London: Herbert Press, 1981)

Payne, Christopher *The Price Guide to 19th Century European Furniture (Excluding British)* (Woodbridge, Suffolk: Antique Collectors' Club, 1988)

Pradère, Alexandre *French Furniture Makers: The Art of the Ébéniste from Louis XIV to the Revolution* (London: Sotheby's, 1989)

Roe, Fred *A History of Oak Furniture* (London: The Connoisseur, 1920)

Sheraton, Thomas *The Cabinet Maker and Upholsterer's Drawing Book,* 3rd edn (1802; repr. New York: Dover, 1972)

Stewart, Janice S. *The Folk Arts of Norway,* 2nd edn (New York: Dover, 1972)

The Treasures of Tutankhamun (London: British Museum, 1972)

Umney, Nick, and Rivers, Shayne *Conservation of Furniture and Related Wooden Objects* (Oxford, England, and Burlington, MA: Architectural Press, 2003)

Veenendaal, Jan *Furniture from Indonesia, Sri Lanka and India during the Dutch Period* (Delft: Volkenkundig Museum Nusantara, 1985)

PLACES TO VISIT

Arundel Castle
West Sussex, England
www.arundelcastle.org

Ashmolean Museum
Oxford, England
www.ashmol.ox.ac.uk

Gallery of the History of the Gillow Manufactory
Judges' Lodgings Museum, Lancaster, England
www.priory.lancs.ac.uk/judges_l_5.html

Geffrye Museum
London, England
www.geffrye-museum.org.uk

Harewood House
near Leeds, England
www.harewood.org

Hildesheim Treasure
Altes Museum, Berlin, Germany
www.smb.spk-berlin.de/ant/e/s.html

Knole House
Kent, England
www.nationaltrust.org.uk/places/knole

La Charité-sur Loire
Nièvre, France
www.ville-la-charite-sur-loire.fr/anglais/musee.htm

Mary Rose and Mary Rose Museum
Portsmouth, England
www.maryrose.org

Musée des Arts Décoratifs
Paris, France
www.paris.org/musees/decoratifs

Musée d'Orsay
Paris, France
www.musee-orsay.fr

Museo Arcivescovile
Ravenna, Italy
www.turismo.ravenna.it/eng/monumenti/619/htm

Museum of Welsh Life
St Fagans, Cardiff, Wales
www.nmgw.ac.uk/mwl

Österreichisches Museum für Angewandte Kunst
Vienna, Austria
www.mak.at

Royal Pavilion
Brighton, East Sussex, England
www.royalpavilion.org.uk

Sotheby's
New York, USA and London, England
www.sothebys.com

Temple Newsam House
Leeds, England
www.leeds.gov.uk/templenewsam

Thonet Museum
Frankenberg/Eder, Germany
www.my-thonet.de/en/museum00.shtml

Victoria and Albert Museum
London, England
www.vam.ac.uk

Weald and Downland Open Air Museum
Singleton, West Sussex, England
www.wealddown.co.uk

Westminster Abbey
London, England
www.westminster-abbey.org

ABOUT THE AUTHOR

Michael Huntley's parents were cataloguers and valuers, and he was brought up in an antique shop. He has always had an interest in woodwork, converting a part of the garden shed into a workshop at the age of 11. After school he joined Sotheby's in London, where he stayed for three years. He then moved to a local general saleroom in Surrey, where he was responsible for producing an antique sale catalogue every four weeks. In 1984, wishing to work on furniture rather than describe it in catalogues, he trained with Bruce Luckhurst as a furniture conservator and restorer. After running his own business for a few years he helped set up Sotheby's Furniture Restoration Workshops in Billingshurst, West Sussex, where he was Head of Department until 1998. He left Sotheby's to work on his own again, and he and his wife Sue bought a piece of land in Wiltshire on which they have built their own house.

Michael now runs his own workshop restoring antiques and making one-off commissions, as well as teaching on the well-respected Conservation and Restoration of Antique Furniture course at West Dean College, West Sussex. He also undertakes consultancy and vetting work, and advises several international collectors. He is a Fellow of the Royal Society for the Encouragement of Arts, Manufactures & Commerce.

Michael can be contacted at huntleyconsultancy.com.

INDEX